What the Work Asks

What the Work Asks

Moral Injury, Repair, and Staying Human in Disaster Response

G. C. Smith

RESOURCE *Publications* • Eugene, Oregon

WHAT THE WORK ASKS
Moral Injury, Repair, and Staying Human in Disaster Response

Resource Publications
An Imprint of Wipf and Stock Publishers
199 W. 8th Ave., Suite 3
Eugene, OR 97401

www.wipfandstock.com

PAPERBACK ISBN: 979-8-3852-8062-9
HARDCOVER ISBN: 979-8-3852-8063-6
EBOOK ISBN: 979-8-3852-8064-3

VERSION NUMBER 03/27/26

For those who showed up when it mattered,
and stayed present when presence was all
that could be offered.

For the responders who carried more than their share,
often without language, permission, or relief.

For those who are still in the work,
those who have stepped back,
and those who are still deciding what
staying will ask of them.

And for the moments of care that did not fix everything,
but mattered anyway.

Contents

Chapter 1—What the Work Asks of You | 1
Chapter 2—The First Time You Notice the Cost | 13
Chapter 3—When the Work Violates What You Believe | 22
Chapter 4—The Culture Around the Work | 37
Chapter 5—How Responders Learn to Survive | 50
Chapter 6—When Survival Stops Being Enough | 62
Chapter 7—The Weight of Repetition | 72
Chapter 8—Leadership and Moral Exposure | 86
Chapter 9—Team Dynamics and Shared Strain | 99
Chapter 10—What Leaders Hold Back | 110
Chapter 11—Staying Without Disappearing | 123
Chapter 12—Repair Is Not a Program | 137
Chapter 13—Telling the Truth About the Cost | 151
Chapter 14—Staying, Leaving, and Staying Changed | 159
Chapter 15—What Remains | 170

A Few Questions to Ponder | 181
Acknowledgements | 185
About the Author | 189

Chapter 1—What the Work Asks of You

You arrive knowing you cannot fix this.

You don't say that out loud. You wouldn't. But you know it the moment you step inside. The smell hits first—damp carpet, bleach, something spoiled that no one has had time to deal with yet. The house is still standing, which already places this family in a category the system understands as less urgent. Standing structures don't photograph well. They don't make compelling statistics. They suggest survival, even when survival feels provisional.

They brought you here because you are supposed to be good at this part. Not logistics, not paperwork, not decisions.

Presence.

She sits at the table with her hands wrapped around a mug she hasn't touched. Someone must have offered it earlier—coffee, maybe, or tea. It's gone cold. She hasn't noticed. The mug gives her something to hold that isn't her own body. It anchors her to the chair in a way words can't.

A man stands near the window, looking outside as if what happened might still be happening, or as if the answer might still be there, waiting to be discovered. You've learned not to rush this moment. People don't look out windows because they expect help to arrive. They look because they don't yet know where else to put their eyes.

You introduce yourself. You say your name, even though the name barely matters. You say what you're here to do. You keep your voice steady, because you've learned how important that is. A steady voice tells people the world hasn't completely come apart, even when everything else suggests otherwise.

They tell you what happened, even though you already know the outline. There was a storm. There was water. There was no warning that felt like enough warning. They talk in fragments, doubling back, correcting themselves. You don't interrupt. Facts are not the point. Accuracy is not the point. This is about making sense of something that still doesn't feel real.

At some point she stops talking and looks at you. This is the moment nobody prepares you for—not because it's dramatic, but because it's quiet. She isn't asking for anything specific. Not money or supplies or answers. She's looking at you the way people look when they're deciding whether it's safe to tell the truth about how bad it really is. The question in her eyes is not what will happen next, but whether she will be alone in it.

You feel the familiar urge rise—the urge to say something useful, something comforting, something that moves the moment forward. You've been trained to help. You've been praised for action. Silence can feel like failure if you're not careful, so you practice not speaking. You've learned, through years of getting it wrong, that this moment does not want movement. It wants witness.

So you sit. You let the silence stretch. You let it ask something of you without trying to meet that demand with words. You feel the pressure in your own chest, the instinct to relieve it by filling the space, and you resist.

She starts crying, but not the kind of crying that needs to be stopped—the kind that needs room. You shift closer without touching. You've learned that too. Touch is not always welcome, even when it's offered with care. Presence is not the same as proximity.

You think, briefly, about how strange it is that this is considered a role—how presence is something organizations deploy like a resource, how it has a line on an org chart. You push the thought aside. This is not the time to reflect on systems. This is the time to stay.

The man turns from the window and asks, "What do we do now?"

It's an honest question, and it deserves an honest answer. The honest answer is that you don't know. You know what the system will do. You know what might come later. You know the timelines and the probabilities and the usual gaps. You know what help might arrive and what almost certainly won't. You also know that none of that is what he's asking. He's asking how to live inside what just happened.

You choose your words carefully. You talk about today, not the future—about food and rest, about not making big decisions yet. You don't promise help you can't guarantee. You don't say things will be okay. You say, "You don't have to figure everything out today."

It feels thin. It always does. Later, you will think about that sentence and wish it were more honest. Tomorrow won't be easier, or the day after that. You know how quickly attention fades. You know how long recovery actually takes, even when no one wants to hear that yet. But right now, the sentence holds just enough truth to be bearable.

They thank you when you leave. That part never gets easier. They thank you for listening, for sitting, for being there. You accept it because refusing gratitude creates its own harm, but something in you tightens every time. Gratitude in these moments often feels misdirected, like credit given to the wrong person. You did not give them what they need; you gave them what you had.

In the car, you sit for a moment before turning the key. You notice your shoulders are up near your ears and lower them deliberately. You take a breath. You tell yourself what you've told yourself before: This is enough. This is what I'm here to do. Then you drive to the next stop.

You are standing in a hallway that was never meant to hold this many people.

Cots line the walls, close enough that you have to turn sideways to pass. Handwritten signs are taped to classroom doors—Restroom. Supplies. Staff Only. The tape is already peeling. Nothing about this place is designed to last. Temporary solutions have a way of becoming semi-permanent, especially when resources thin.

A woman steps into your path. She doesn't grab you. She does it gently, like someone trying not to be a problem. You notice that before she speaks. People who have been displaced often apologize with their bodies before they use words.

"They said you might know," she says, hope disguised as politeness.

She tells you about her mother—elderly, diabetic, medications left behind in the evacuation. She's been asking all day, patient in the way people are patient when they feel they have no other option. You already know where this is going.

You know what resources exist. You know the process. You know which answers are technically correct. You also know none of them will feel like help. You know the difference between explanation and relief. You listen anyway. You ask questions you already know the answers to, because the asking itself matters. It tells her this story is being heard by a human being, not absorbed by a system. It tells her she is not invisible, even if the outcome will be the same.

When you explain, you keep your voice even. You talk about what can happen, not what won't. You explain timelines without committing to them. You avoid definitive no's as long as you can. You know how fragile hope is, even when it's unrealistic.

She follows every word. At the end, there is a pause. "So," she says slowly, "there's nothing you can do right now."

It isn't anger or accusation. It's clarity.

You meet her eyes and say the thing you hate saying. "Not right now." She exhales and looks past you, down the hallway full of people waiting. When she looks back, her voice is softer. "Okay," she says. "Thank you for explaining."

She thanks you again. You watch her walk away and feel something recoil inside you. Gratitude offered in these moments always feels misplaced. You didn't solve anything. You translated scarcity into gentler language. You stood between her and a system that cannot respond quickly enough.

Later, someone on your team makes a joke meant to lighten the mood—something about how everyone thinks you have magic answers. People laugh. You laugh too, because that's what you do when the alternative would make the room uncomfortable. The laughter sits wrong.

Being the face of limitation does something to you. It's not just that you deliver bad news. It's that you absorb the emotional impact of decisions made far away, by people who will never meet the woman in the hallway. You carry those moments with you.

It happens faster than you expect. One moment you're explaining a process. The next, the room changes temperature.

The man's voice rises in steps, each sentence sharper than the last. You notice people nearby growing quiet, watching without looking like they're watching. Someone shifts a chair back, just in case.

"I've been here all day," he says. "All day."

You nod. You don't interrupt. Interrupting would escalate things, and you know that. You've been trained for moments like this. De-escalation is a skill you didn't realize you'd need when you first entered this work.

He gestures around the room—toward the tables, the cots, the signs taped to the walls, toward you. "You keep saying there's a process," he says. "But the process isn't helping."

He's right.

You feel the familiar tightening in your chest, the instinct to defend, to clarify, to explain constraints. You swallow it. This isn't about accuracy. This is about containment. Anger, when it has nowhere to go, looks for a body to land in.

"I hear how angry you are," you say, keeping your voice low and even. You notice you've made yourself smaller without meaning to.

He steps closer. "Do you?" he asks.

This is the moment when anger looks for a target, and you are the closest one available. You didn't design the system. You didn't set the limits. You didn't decide how resources would be allocated. But you are standing here. You are wearing the badge. You are speaking the language of the response.

You absorb it.

He tells you everything that has gone wrong—some of it true, some distorted by exhaustion and fear. None of it malicious. It's pain with nowhere else to go. You let him finish. When he finally stops, breathing hard, the room is very quiet.

Later, someone checks in on you. "You handled that well," they say. You nod. You know the script.

What no one asks is where the anger went. It didn't disappear. It passed through you.

You don't notice it while you're still working. During the response, you are steady. You make decisions. You listen. You move from one need to the next with little space in between. The structure holds you up. Urgency does its job.

It's later, when the structure is gone, that the weight shows up.

You are driving home on familiar roads your body knows without asking your mind. The radio is on low, then off. At a stoplight, you notice your hands are shaking.

At home, everything is where you left it—shoes by the door, mail on the counter, a light left on in a room you didn't use that morning. The normalcy feels almost offensive. You move through the space like a guest.

Someone asks how it went. This question is harder than it should be. You give the answer you've practiced—It was a long day, or It was intense, or People lost a lot. You choose something neutral, something that won't require translation. They nod. They mean well. The conversation moves on.

Later, when you're alone, the images return in fragments. Not the dramatic ones, but the small ones: the mug gone cold, the hallway lined with cots, the way a woman's shoulders dropped when you said not right now.

You replay conversations, searching for alternate endings. You know, rationally, that none of those changes would have altered the outcome. The system would still be the system. The limits would still be there. Rational knowledge does not quiet the questions.

In the morning, you wake already tired. Your body feels wired and heavy at the same time. You are less patient with small inconveniences. A slow cashier irritates you. A minor complaint feels outsized. You catch yourself thinking something you don't like: You have no idea how bad it can get.

The thought scares you. You don't want to become that person. You've seen them—people who stay long enough that empathy thins, that cynicism hardens into armor. You promised yourself you wouldn't let that happen.

So you reset. You exercise. You eat well. You do the things you know you're supposed to do. They help, but only on the surface. Underneath, something remains unsettled. It isn't fear or sadness or even anger, exactly. It's the sense that you were asked to stand in for something larger than yourself, and that the stand-in never fully ends.

The next time it happens, you recognize the feeling immediately. Different disaster. Different location. Same role.

You're walking toward another temporary site, clipboard in hand, already rehearsing what you'll say. With mild surprise, you realize you already know how this day will feel—not the details, but the shape. You will listen. You will explain. You will say not yet, or not here, or I don't know. You will be thanked.

The recognition doesn't stop you from doing the work. It changes how you enter it. You brace—not dramatically, just a small internal adjustment. You keep your voice professional. You manage your expectations. You don't let yourself imagine outcomes that rarely arrive.

Someone asks how you're doing. "Fine," you say. It's mostly true. You are functioning, competent, useful. You are also quieter than you used to be. This isn't collapse. It's adaptation, and you don't yet realize that adaptation has a direction.

Later still, you are the site manager.

You didn't plan to become one. You stayed long enough, showed enough steadiness, absorbed enough, and one day the role shifted. Now you are responsible not just for presence, but for decisions.

The building is too small. The line is too long. Supplies are limited. Staff are tired. You feel the weight of every variable at once. You stand with supervisors reviewing numbers that never feel like people until they do—capacity, staffing, safety. You know the language. You also know what the language will mean when it lands on the floor.

"We need to close intake by six," someone says.

You nod. The decision makes sense. It is defensible. It is also going to hurt.

When you announce it, the room goes quiet in the way rooms do when people sense bad news before it's spoken. You explain carefully, using the words you've learned to use, avoiding unnecessary finality.

A man near the back raises his hand. "Where are we supposed to go?"

You answer honestly. You give options. You do not lie. He doesn't argue. He just nods slowly, like someone filing something away.

Afterward, a staff member tells you that you handled it well. They mean it as praise. It lands like weight.

That night, you lie awake replaying the decision—not because it was wrong, but because it was necessary, and because it will live somewhere in you now. You understand, in a new way, that leadership doesn't protect you from moral cost. It concentrates it.

You notice it during a meeting—no raised voices, no visible conflict, just updates delivered efficiently. Someone mentions a decision made earlier in the day, a good decision by most measures, necessary and defensible. You feel something in your gut resist.

You wait for someone else to say it. They don't.

You clear your throat and speak carefully, framing it as a question. "I'm wondering about the impact on the families who were turned away this morning."

There's a pause—long enough to register, not hostile. Someone offers an explanation. Someone else nods. The conversation moves on. No one engages the question you were actually asking.

Later, you try again with a colleague you trust. You're more direct this time. They listen, nod, say, "Yeah. That's tough," and then change the subject.

You don't blame them. Everyone is carrying too much already. Still, something shifts. You realize some parts of this work have nowhere to land—not because they're inappropriate, but because there's no space designed to hold them. So you begin to carry them quietly, not out of fear but out of efficiency.

You may recognize these moments—not because they are extraordinary, but because they are ordinary in a way that doesn't get talked about. They don't look like crisis or feel like failure. They repeat quietly over time.

Most people are taught to understand cost in this work as exhaustion or stress. Rest is offered. Boundaries are encouraged. Sometimes that helps. Sometimes it doesn't touch the thing that's actually bothering you.

What these moments share is responsibility—not formal responsibility, but human responsibility: being the one who stands in front of someone when the answer is incomplete; being thanked for showing up when what's needed is more than presence can provide.

This kind of responsibility doesn't announce itself. That's why it's easy to miss. The cost shows up as narrowing, guarding, bracing before conversations that used to feel open.

You may tell yourself this is experience. It is. But experience is not neutral. When it accumulates without being named, it leaves residue.

This book is not here to tell you the work is wrong. It is here to say the work is morally demanding in ways rarely acknowledged, and that demand has a cost. There is language for what happens when people are asked, again and again, to act with care inside systems that cannot fully honor that care.

We will get to that language. For now, it's enough to say this: if you recognized yourself here, you are not alone, and you are not failing at the work. You are responding to what the work asks of you.

Chapter 2—**The First Time You Notice the Cost**

The Pause

The first sign is small enough that you almost miss it.

You're packing for a response you've done dozens of times before. The call came late the night before—storm damage, displacement, a temporary shelter opening within hours. Nothing about it is unusual, and that's part of what unsettles you later. There's no dramatic trigger, no sense this response will be different from the others.

Your bag is half packed before you're fully awake: boots, gloves, the jacket with the patch that tells people who you are when you arrive. You use the same checklist you always do, because forgetting something costs time, and time is never neutral in the field.

You move automatically—until you don't.

Your hand pauses over the last item, just for a second. Long enough to register, not long enough to alarm you. No one watching would notice, but you do. It isn't dread or fear. It doesn't even feel emotional in a way you recognize. It feels like weight, like something pressing lightly but insistently on the moment.

You stand there longer than necessary, trying to identify the hesitation. You've handled worse. You know the role. You trust yourself in these environments. You've built a life around being reliable in precisely this way, so you finish packing and keep moving.

On the drive in, you tell yourself you're tired—the late call, the short night, the cumulative wear of back-to-back responses. That explanation works, mostly. Familiar explanations are comforting.

The sun is barely up when you arrive. The parking lot is already filling. People stand in loose clusters near the entrance, some with bags, some with nothing. Staff move quickly, but there's an edge to it—the kind of motion that comes from making decisions before there's enough information.

You step into your role without effort. You answer questions, orient volunteers, translate uncertainty into something usable. You explain what will happen next, even when you know it may change in an hour. You are calm, competent, present, and people trust you almost immediately.

You notice how easy that still is, and then you notice something else: you're scanning differently. Not just for needs, but for where conversations might turn hard, where frustration might peak, where you'll need to step in before voices rise or hope drops too fast. You've always been observant. This feels more like bracing.

Mid-morning, someone asks a question you've answered countless times. They aren't upset, just confused, trying to understand a process that doesn't look like they expected. Irritation flickers before you can stop it, and it surprises you. The reaction is small and fleeting. You answer kindly and professionally. You don't let it show. Still, you feel it register, like a warning light you didn't expect to see.

That wasn't necessary, you think.

Not the question. The reaction.

You file it away and keep moving.

By lunchtime, you realize you haven't eaten. You grab something quickly, standing while you eat, scanning the room out of habit. Even when you sit, part of you stays alert. You notice where voices rise, where someone looks close to tears. You tell yourself this is focus. It is. It's also vigilance.

Later, someone thanks you. "You're really good at this," they say. "You don't seem rattled at all." You smile. You know how to accept that kind of comment. Steadiness matters here, but inside, the word rattled echoes longer than it should.

The day winds down. The site quiets. You close things up and make notes. Everything that needs doing gets done. You leave tired but functional, the way you always have.

It's later, when the day is officially over, that the pause returns. Not urgently or dramatically—just as you're getting ready for bed. Your body is tired, but your mind is still moving, replaying fragments and scanning for what you might have missed. You think about the hesitation that morning. You hadn't thought about it all day. Now it's there again—quiet, insistent.

You don't know what it means. You only know it didn't used to be there, and that knowledge settles differently than fatigue ever has.

A few days later, it shows up again, not during anything dramatic. You're standing in a grocery store, staring at a shelf longer than necessary, choosing between two versions of the same thing. You've done this a thousand times. This time, your body doesn't move.

Just a hesitation—the same one from packing your bag, the same pause before speaking in the debrief. You stand there long enough that someone reaches around you.

"Sorry," you say automatically. The word comes too easily.

You grab something at random and move on, irritated with yourself. You tell yourself you're distracted, that your mind is still catching up. At checkout, you notice your shoulders are tight. You drop them deliberately and breathe out. It helps. It doesn't clear the feeling.

At home, someone asks about the response. Not probing, just curious.

"How was it?"

You open your mouth—and hesitate again. You could give the usual summary: busy, long days, hard stories. You know how to shape it so it doesn't worry anyone. You start to say it, then stop.

"I don't know how to explain it," you say instead. The sentence surprises you.

They wait. You feel the pull to resolve the moment, to offer something neat and finished. You don't. After a pause, you say, "It was fine. I just . . . noticed something."

"What kind of something?"

You think about the pause, the irritation, the way the day followed you home. "I don't think I used to feel it like this."

They nod gently, as if that's enough. You feel relieved and unsettled at the same time.

That night, you lie awake longer than usual. Not replaying scenes, just aware. You notice how easily your body shifts into alertness without any external cue, how often your mind drifts back toward the field. You've always been capable of this. You've relied on it.

This feels different—less like readiness and more like residue.

Life resumes its rhythms: work, home, small conversations. You function normally. No one would think anything is wrong. You don't think anything is wrong either.

But you keep noticing. You choose words more carefully than necessary. You scan rooms that don't require scanning. You anticipate disappointment where you didn't used to. None of it disrupts your life. That's what makes it harder to dismiss.

You run into a colleague by chance, someone who's been doing this work about as long as you have. "Do you ever feel like something sticks with you now that didn't used to?" you ask.

They pause—just briefly. "Yeah," they say.

They don't elaborate. Neither do you. The moment passes. It shouldn't matter.

It does.

On the next response, you catch the noticing in real time. You're listening to someone explain their situation, fully present, doing the work exactly as trained. Underneath it, you're aware of the cost as it accrues—not afterward, but during.

The awareness doesn't stop you or slow you down. It just exists alongside the work.

You realize you're now doing two things at once: responding, and tracking what responding is doing to you. That's new.

At the end of the day, you write your notes carefully and close the file. You sit longer than required. You don't feel dramatic or undone. You feel changed—not enough to name, but enough to notice.

This is how it starts for most people—not with collapse, but with awareness. With the sense that the work has begun to leave a mark that doesn't wash off at the end of the day, with the realization that you're no longer moving through these spaces untouched. You don't draw conclusions. You don't make plans. You carry the knowledge forward.

Something is different now, and you don't yet know what that will ask of you.

The Moment You Don't Say It

The next response doesn't announce itself as important either. A temporary assistance center, folding tables, paper signs taped to walls, lines longer than planned. Everyone is doing their best inside a strained system.

You've been here before. You know the rhythm—where confusion builds, which questions come first and which come later, when patience thins.

A family sits across from you, exhausted but composed. They apologize for taking your time. You tell them they don't need to. As you review their paperwork, you already know the outcome. The criteria are clear, the margins narrow. Nothing here will open the door they're hoping for.

You slow your pace anyway. You explain carefully, watch their faces, leave space for questions. They don't interrupt. When you finish, silence lingers.

"So," one of them says, "there's nothing."

"There's nothing available through this program," you say, qualifying the sentence. You explain referrals and describe possibilities that may or may not open later. They listen.

"I just wanted to make sure we didn't do something wrong," the other adult says.

"You didn't," you say immediately, and you mean it. They did everything asked of them. That's part of what makes this harder.

They thank you and leave quietly. You sit with the file longer than necessary, rereading details you know by heart. Nothing has changed.

A colleague asks if you're okay. "I'm fine," you say. It's true in a narrow sense.

Later, during a brief debrief, someone mentions how hard the day has been. You consider saying something—not venting, just naming how often you're asked to be the human face of limits you didn't choose. You open your mouth, then close it.

There isn't space. There isn't time. There isn't a clear next step.

So you stay quiet.

The meeting ends. You feel relief, and you feel something else—a faint sense of loss that doesn't attach to any single moment. That night, the family returns in fragments: not the conversation itself, but impressions, the care they took to stay composed.

You realize there was something you didn't say—not because it would have changed anything, but because it was true:

This shouldn't be this way.

You didn't say it. The realization settles quietly, and it doesn't disappear.

Recognition Without Language

After that, the noticing becomes harder to turn off. You prepare for disappointment before it arrives, listen while already mapping limits, rehearse explanations in advance. This makes you efficient. It also changes how the work feels.

You manage expectations more than outcomes, soften hope early so it doesn't break later. You call it realism, and you still notice the shift. The noticing follows you home. You compare problems without meaning to and feel a flicker of guilt. It isn't judgment; it's saturation. Your internal scale has recalibrated.

A colleague checks in. "How are you holding up?" You hesitate longer than expected and give a true-enough answer—tired, long days. You don't mention what lingers. After the call, you notice how much effort it took to stay on the surface.

You start to see patterns. Irritation comes faster. Patience thins earlier. Ambiguity feels heavier. Nothing extreme, just different. Rest helps your body. Time off helps your schedule.

Neither touches this.

The first time you encounter the phrase moral injury, it doesn't feel immediately relevant. It's in an article or a training meant for another field. You almost skip it, but something makes you pause. It isn't about trauma exposure. It's about what happens when people are required to act against their values, or are prevented from acting in accordance with them, especially under constraint.

You feel the same quiet recognition—the pause, the silence, the residue. You don't adopt the language. You let it sit.

At first, you try to address what you're feeling the usual way: better boundaries, more rest, a little time off. It helps. It doesn't resolve this, because this isn't about energy.

It's about alignment.

Looking back, you'll see this as a threshold—not the moment you were injured, but the moment you noticed the cost, the moment you stopped assuming the work was neutral. You didn't have language yet. You didn't need it.

You noticed.

And once you noticed, you couldn't unnotice it.

Chapter 3—**When the Work Violates What You Believe**

You Did Everything Right

The checklist is complete.

You've reviewed intake notes, verified eligibility, confirmed available resources. You've checked the timeline twice to make sure you didn't miss a deadline that would change the outcome. Everything lines up the way it's supposed to. You did everything right. That's what makes this harder than if something had gone wrong.

The woman sitting across from you is older than you expected—not elderly, but worn in the way people get when they've been holding too much for too long. She keeps smoothing the edge of the folder in her lap, even though the papers inside are already neat. She's prepared. She's done what she was told. You recognize that posture: hope restrained by caution.

You explain the process again, slowly, even though you've already done it once. You watch her face closely as you speak, looking for confusion, for questions, for the moment where the words stop making sense. She follows you, and that almost makes you wish she wouldn't.

When you reach the end, you pause. This is where the conversation usually turns—where people push back or argue or cry, where you sometimes get to advocate, bend something slightly, find a workaround.

None of that is available today.

You tell her she doesn't meet the criteria. Not harshly or abruptly. You say it with care. You explain why. You reference policy, timelines, categories created far away from this room. She listens. She nods. For a moment, neither of you speaks.

"So," she says finally, "there's nothing."

You feel the familiar tightening in your chest. "There's not assistance through this program," you say, choosing your words carefully. You don't say nothing. You offer referrals, phone numbers, possibilities that might help later—or might not help at all.

She looks down at her folder, then back up at you. "I did everything they told me to do," she says. Not accusing. Just stating a fact.

You nod. "I know," you say—and you do. You know she followed instructions. You know she showed up on time, waited in line, answered questions honestly. You know she trusted the process.

You also know it didn't matter.

She closes the folder carefully, as if the order of the papers still counts for something. She thanks you for explaining. She stands. Before she leaves, she hesitates.

"I'm glad someone listened," she says.

That sentence lands harder than anything else.

After she goes, you sit for a moment longer than necessary. You review the file again, even though you know the outcome won't change. You look for something you might have missed—some small detail that could reopen the door.

There isn't one.

You didn't fail. That's the problem.

Later that day, someone tells you that you handled the case well. They mean it sincerely. You nod and accept the comment. You've learned that deflecting praise can create awkwardness, and awkwardness slows things down.

You move on to the next person, but something has shifted—nothing dramatic, just enough that you notice it. You're more careful with your tone. You keep explanations tighter. You avoid inviting questions that will only lead back to the same answer. You do this without conscious intention. It's efficient. It protects time.

It also protects you.

At the end of the day, you complete your notes. You document the interaction accurately. You record the decision. You close the file. Everything is in order.

On the drive home, the woman's sentence repeats itself without asking permission: I did everything they told me to do. You find yourself responding to it internally: So did I.

The thought unsettles you.

In the days that follow, the moment doesn't resolve the way others have. It doesn't fade with rest or disappear when the next response begins. It lingers quietly, resurfacing when you least expect it—when someone asks why a program has limits, when a colleague says, "At least we're helping some people," when you hear yourself explain, again, that this is how the system works.

You don't disagree. You just feel the distance between working and being right widen slightly.

You begin to notice how often you rely on procedure to carry the weight of decisions you wish didn't belong to you. Procedure gives you cover. It gives you language. It gives you a way to speak without saying what you actually feel.

Most days, that's enough. Some days, it isn't.

The next time something similar happens, you feel it sooner. You recognize the sensation as you're speaking, not after—a small internal recoil, a tightening behind the sternum, a sense that you are participating in something that violates your sense of fairness even as you perform it competently.

You don't stop. You can't. You also don't forget.

You notice how quickly you move to justification: If it weren't me, it would be someone else. The policy exists for a reason. I didn't design the system. All of those things are true.

None of them touch the feeling.

What's difficult about moments like this is how ordinary they are. There is no crisis, no raised voices, no ethical drama that would justify escalation. Just a quiet misalignment between what you believe should happen and what you are required to enforce.

You can live with that once. You can live with it twice. It's when it becomes routine that something starts to wear—not your skills.

Your trust.

You don't talk about this with your team. There doesn't seem to be a place for it. Debriefs focus on numbers and flow. Supervisors want to know what can be improved next time. Wellness check-ins ask if you're resting enough.

None of those questions are wrong. None of them reach this.

So you file it away with other moments that don't quite fit anywhere. You tell yourself it's part of the job. You're right.

You just haven't yet asked what the job is doing in return.

The recognition comes later, quietly, when you're explaining the work to someone outside it. They ask what's hardest. You start to say something about hours, or funding, or logistics. Halfway through the sentence, you stop.

"That's not it," you say, surprised by your own certainty.

You search for words. "It's when you know what would be right," you say slowly, "and you can't do it."

You hear yourself say it and realize how long you've been carrying that sentence without knowing it.

This is often where the work begins to change—not outwardly, but inwardly. You start to feel the weight of alignment, or the lack of it. You notice when actions and values diverge. You feel it in your body before you can articulate it.

You don't yet have a name for this. You just know that doing everything right doesn't always feel right, and that knowledge, once acquired, doesn't leave you.

The Decision Was Already Made

You can tell before the meeting starts—not from anything someone says, but from the arrangement of the room. The chairs are set. The agenda is already printed. The conversation begins five minutes late but somehow still feels rushed. You've been in enough of these rooms to recognize the signs.

The decision exists. The meeting is about how to carry it out.

You take a seat near the end of the table, not because you were told to, but because you've learned where your voice lands most safely. Close enough to be heard, far enough to observe. You set your notebook down even though you're not sure what you'll write.

The first few items move quickly: updates, numbers, timelines. Everything sounds reasonable. No one is careless. No one is acting in bad faith.

That almost makes it harder.

Then the plan is presented. It's clean, efficient, within policy. It solves several problems at once. You can see why it was chosen. You can also see exactly who it will affect, and you feel it in your body before your mind finishes the thought—a tightening, a familiar internal resistance. You already know how this will land in the field.

You wait. Someone else will say it, you think. Someone with more authority, someone whose role includes asking these questions.

No one does.

The discussion moves forward into implementation details: staffing needs, messaging, optics. Someone suggests phrasing that will "set expectations." You watch the conversation narrow and glance down at your notes, even though the page is still blank.

This is the moment. You know it.

When you speak, you do it carefully. You frame your concern in neutral language. You reference impact, not morality. You talk about families, not principles. You choose words that fit the room.

"I'm concerned about how this will affect people who don't meet these criteria but are still significantly impacted," you say.

The sentence is measured, reasonable—the tone you've practiced over years. The room goes quiet, just briefly. Someone responds with data. Another mentions capacity. A third reminds the group of constraints you all already know.

No one argues with you. No one follows you either.

The conversation moves on. You sit back, nod at the right moments, make a note or two so it looks like you're engaged. Outwardly, nothing has changed.

Inwardly, something settles. You understand the outcome will not shift.

The decision was already made.

After the meeting, a colleague catches up with you in the hallway. "You're right," they say quietly. "I just don't think there was room to change it."

You appreciate the honesty. You also feel the familiar loneliness of being right without being able to act on it. They aren't dismissing you or disagreeing. They're naming reality. You nod. "I get it," you say.

And you do.

Understanding doesn't bring relief.

In the days that follow, you're the one who helps implement the plan. You help draft talking points. You answer questions. You absorb reactions. You listen as people express confusion and frustration and disbelief.

You don't lie. You also don't tell the whole truth. You tell the version of the truth that keeps the system moving.

When someone asks why the decision was made, you explain constraints: limited resources, fairness at scale, what can be done—not what can't. You do this well.

That's what makes the weight heavier.

At one point, someone says, "But that doesn't make sense."

You pause. They're right. You know it, they know it. The sense it makes is administrative, not human. You explain again, choosing slightly different words. You watch their face as the explanation lands, as disappointment replaces confusion. They don't argue. They just look tired.

You feel the urge to say something else—something honest that acknowledges the gap. You don't.

You are not authorized to speak that way here.

Later, when the room is empty, you sit at the table where the conversation took place. The chairs are pushed in. The floor has been cleaned. Nothing about the space holds what happened there.

You notice how easy it would be for this moment to disappear if you let it. You could frame it as a tough but necessary decision. You could tell yourself your responsibility ended when the meeting did. You could move on.

You've done that before.

This time, you don't quite manage it.

You keep thinking about how quickly moral weight gets redistributed in settings like this—how decisions made collectively land individually, how the cost concentrates on those closest to the impact. You think about how often you are asked to carry that concentration quietly.

The hardest part isn't that the decision stands. It's that no one names what it costs—not the people who made it, not the people who enforce it, not the people who live with it.

Cost remains abstract. You feel it concretely.

You notice that after meetings like this, you change how you speak in future ones. You raise fewer concerns unless you're certain they will land. You save your voice for moments you think matter most. You learn to read the room faster.

This looks like maturity. In some ways, it is. In other ways, it's retreat. You aren't withdrawing from the work.

You're withdrawing from the risk of being morally exposed without effect.

Later, when you describe this job to someone new, you emphasize collaboration and teamwork. You talk about shared responsibility and highlight how decisions are rarely made by one person alone. All of that is true.

You leave out the part where shared responsibility can also mean shared evasion, where no single person feels accountable for the moral outcome because everyone participated just enough.

You don't say that out loud.

You carry it.

This is one of the ways moral injury deepens—not through dramatic conflict, but through repeated experiences of seeing clearly and being unable to act meaningfully. Of speaking carefully and being heard but not heeded. Of understanding why things are the way they are and still feeling that they shouldn't be.

You begin to recognize that your role often places you at the intersection of knowledge and power without granting you much of either.

That position is exhausting.

You leave the building at the end of the day with the familiar mix of resolve and weariness. You will return tomorrow. You will do the work. You will show up.

You always do.

What you don't yet know is how many times you can stand in rooms like that before something essential begins to dull. That recognition comes later.

You Carry It Home

You don't feel it right away, and that's one of the things that makes it confusing. The meeting ends. The site closes. The workday resolves into tasks completed and boxes checked. You pack up your materials, say the right goodbyes, promise to follow up where follow-up is possible, and walk out into the parking lot with the rest of the team.

Everything looks normal, and you tell yourself this is good. Normal means contained. Normal means you did what you came to do and can now let it go.

You don't yet realize the work has followed you.

On the drive home, your body stays alert longer than necessary. Your shoulders remain tight. Your jaw aches slightly, though you can't remember clenching it. You turn the radio on, then off. Silence feels better until it doesn't. At a stoplight, a fragment of the day surfaces without warning—not the whole scene, just a sentence, a look on someone's face, the moment you chose one explanation over another. You shake your head, as if that might dislodge it.

You've learned how to leave work at work. Or at least, you thought you had.

At home, nothing reflects the day you just had. The lights come on as expected. The floor is clean. The refrigerator hums quietly. The world inside your front door hasn't been touched by the decisions you made hours earlier.

This should feel grounding.

Instead, it feels dissonant.

You move through the space with efficiency—shoes off, keys down, hands washed. You answer a question about dinner without really hearing it. When someone asks how your day went, you give a version that is technically accurate and emotionally neutral.

"It was busy," you say, or, "It was a long one."

They nod. The conversation moves on. You feel relief and disappointment at the same time.

Later, when you finally sit down, your body registers what your mind has been postponing. It shows up as restlessness, or heaviness, or a vague irritation that doesn't seem connected to anything in particular. You scroll on your phone without absorbing what you're seeing. You start one task, then abandon it for another.

You tell yourself you're just tired.

You are tired.

That's not all of it.

The memory that finally settles in is not the hardest moment of the day. It's the quiet one—the moment after you explained the decision, when the person across from you nodded slowly, as if filing the information away somewhere they didn't want to visit yet. The moment when you could see understanding arrive alongside disappointment.

That look stays with you, not because you did something wrong, but because you did something you didn't believe in.

This is the part that's hardest to explain to people outside the work. They assume the weight comes from exposure to loss or trauma, and sometimes it does. But this feels different. This isn't about what you witnessed.

It's about what you participated in.

You replay the interaction not looking for errors, but looking for escape routes—alternate phrasing, different timing, some small adjustment that might have changed how it landed. You know, rationally, that nothing you said would have changed the outcome.

Rational knowledge doesn't quiet the search.

The next morning, the residue is still there: a dullness where there used to be sharpness, a slight impatience with minor inconveniences, a sense that you are carrying something unfinished. You notice how quickly you move into task mode, how you focus on things that can be completed and resolved. You avoid situations that invite ambiguity—not as pathology, but as strategy. You are unconsciously steering away from moments that will ask you to feel the same dissonance again.

Over time, you recognize the pattern. Certain days follow you home more than others—not the chaotic ones, the constrained ones. The days where you are required to enforce decisions that make sense structurally but violate something you believe about fairness or care.

Those are the days that linger. They show up later when the house is quiet, when you're brushing your teeth, when you're half awake in the early morning and your mind is replaying scenes you thought you'd already set down.

You don't tell anyone about these moments. They don't sound serious enough. They also don't sound like stress in the way people understand stress.

Eventually, you notice a change in how you prepare for the next response. You don't dread it. You don't resist it.

You adjust.

You lower your expectations for alignment. You anticipate the moment when you'll have to say something that doesn't sit right. You prepare language that creates distance without sounding cold. You call this professionalism. In many ways, it is.

You are learning how to survive.

There is a moment, later than you expect, when the cumulative weight becomes visible. It isn't during a response. It's during an ordinary conversation.

Someone asks why you stay in this work. It's a question you've answered many times. You usually talk about purpose, service, showing up.

This time, you hesitate. The words don't come as easily. You still believe in the work; that hasn't changed. What has changed is your awareness of its cost. You realize you don't want to offer a simplified version anymore. You also don't want to burden them with the truth.

So you give a partial answer.

Again.

This is often when people begin to wonder if something is wrong with them—why this feels heavier now, why certain moments linger longer than they used to, why rest doesn't quite restore what's been spent. Without language, the mind looks for explanations.

Maybe I'm burning out. Maybe I need a break. Maybe I'm not cut out for this after all.

Those explanations feel close enough to be convincing.

They're also incomplete.

The first time you encounter the phrase moral injury, it doesn't land with drama. It lands with relief—not relief that something is wrong, but relief that something makes sense. You read a description meant for another context and feel that internal recognition again, the same one you felt when you first noticed the cost.

This isn't about fear. This isn't about trauma exposure. This is about being repeatedly placed in situations where your values are engaged but not honored—where you are required to act, speak, or comply in ways that violate what you believe is right, where the harm is not intentional but real, and where the cost doesn't stay at the site.

Naming it doesn't make the memories disappear. It does something else. It gives you a way to understand why they came home with you in the first place, why they showed up in quiet moments, why they resisted resolution—why they asked to be acknowledged rather than managed.

You realize that what you've been carrying is not just fatigue.

It's moral residue.

Once you see this, you begin to relate to those moments differently. You stop treating them as failures of resilience. You stop scolding yourself for not "letting it go." You begin to understand that these moments followed you home because they had nowhere else to land.

They mattered. They still do.

This does not mean you stop doing the work. It means you stop pretending the work is cost-neutral. You begin to see that staying requires more than endurance. It requires ways of naming, sharing, and repairing what is strained when values and actions diverge.

That work is slower, less visible, often unsupported.

It is also essential.

By the end of this chapter, nothing has been resolved, and that is intentional. What has changed is recognition: you can now see that the quiet weight you carry home is not a personal weakness or a sign that you care too much. It is evidence that you have been doing morally demanding work in constrained systems, and that the cost of that work does not always end when the shift does.

You are not alone in this.

And now, you are no longer unnamed in it.

Chapter 4—The Culture Around the Work

"This Is Just How It Is"

The phrase shows up later—not on your first response, when everything is still new and adrenaline carries you over rough edges. It appears once you've been around long enough to notice patterns, to ask questions, to wonder out loud why the same problems keep repeating.

You hear it the first time when you raise a concern that feels reasonable. You aren't accusing anyone. You're asking about impact—about whether there's another way to handle a recurring situation that keeps putting responders in impossible positions. Someone listens. Someone nods, and then—softly, almost kindly—they say it: "This is just how it is."

At the time, it feels like information. Later, you realize it was instruction.

The situation itself is ordinary: a shelter over capacity, staff stretched thin, volunteers rotating in and out—some trained, some not. Policies are posted on the wall, but they no longer match what's happening on the floor.

A family approaches the desk with a request you've heard before. They need something that makes sense humanly but doesn't fit procedurally. You know the answer before they finish asking, and you also know how much explaining it will take. You glance toward your supervisor, hoping for a signal—some acknowledgment that this is one of those moments where flexibility matters. They meet your eyes briefly, then look away.

You handle it. You always do.

Afterward, you mention it quietly—not as a complaint, but as a pattern. "We're getting this question a lot," you say. "It's putting staff in a tough spot."

Your supervisor exhales. Not irritated. Tired. "I know," they say. "But this is just how it is right now."

Right now stretches longer than you expect.

Culture doesn't announce itself. It forms through repetition—through what gets taken seriously and what gets smoothed over, through what earns time in meetings and what gets handled in hallways, if it gets handled at all. Logistics get attention. Efficiency gets rewarded. Adaptability is praised, especially when it means making do without more support.

Moral distress rarely makes the agenda, and when it does surface, it's reframed quickly—as stress, as personality, as something that can be managed with better self-care. You start to understand there is an expectation to absorb certain costs without naming them. It isn't written anywhere; it's learned.

The longer you stay, the more fluent you become. You learn which questions to ask publicly and which to save for private conversations. You learn how to raise concerns without sounding critical. You learn how to translate ethical discomfort into operational risk, because that language travels farther.

You also learn when not to speak—not because you don't care, but because you already know what will happen. The conversation will stall. The answer will be constraints. The work will continue unchanged. You will have spent energy naming something with nowhere to land.

So you choose efficiency. You tell yourself this is maturity, and in some ways it is.

There's a moment when you catch yourself using the phrase.

A newer responder comes to you with the same concern you once brought to someone else. They're trying to make sense of a decision that feels misaligned with the values they were told the organization holds. You listen. You understand exactly what they're saying. You also know how the system will respond.

You hear yourself say, "Yeah. It's frustrating. But this is just how it is."

The words feel familiar as soon as they leave your mouth. They also feel wrong. You see something shift in their face—not anger, not disappointment exactly, but recalibration. Expectation adjusting to reality. You recognize it because you've lived it. Later, you replay the interaction and wonder whether you helped them or initiated them.

Culture shapes what feels possible, and over time, you notice certain conversations simply don't happen—not because people are hostile, but because they're exhausted, or because they've learned that naming certain tensions doesn't lead anywhere useful.

You rarely hear, "This puts us in a morally impossible position." You hear, "We need to manage expectations." You rarely hear, "This harms responders." You hear, "Make sure you're taking care of yourself." None of those responses are wrong. They're incomplete.

The effect is cumulative. Each time a concern is deflected rather than engaged, something small is reinforced: the idea that this discomfort is normal, expected, part of the job. You internalize that message. You stop looking for alignment. You start looking for endurance. Success becomes measured by the absence of visible breakdown rather than the presence of moral clarity. If no one is complaining, things must be fine. If the site is running, the cost must be acceptable. If responders keep showing up, the system must be working.

You begin to see how silence gets interpreted as consent.

What's hardest is that much of this culture is built with good intentions. Leaders are under pressure. Resources are scarce. Decisions have to be made quickly. There is rarely time to slow down and consider moral impact. Urgency becomes the organizing principle, and urgency leaves little room for anything that doesn't move the work forward. Moral reflection starts to feel like a luxury, so it's deferred—again and again.

During one response, a volunteer breaks down unexpectedly. They aren't new. They've handled hard things before. This one catches them. They step outside, visibly shaken. Someone asks what happened.

"They just took it personally," another volunteer says. "They need thicker skin."

The comment isn't cruel. It's practical. It explains the situation in a way that lets everyone else keep working. You feel a flicker of resistance. You wonder if the volunteer hit a moral limit, not an emotional one—if what they encountered violated something they believed should never be violated. You don't say that. You cover their shift.

The work continues.

Over time, the message becomes clear: feeling too much gets framed as fragility. Questioning decisions gets framed as naïveté. Naming moral conflict gets framed as impractical. Staying requires adaptation, and you adapt. Most people do.

The phrase keeps showing up—in shelters, in meetings, in after-action conversations. "This is just how it is."

It explains everything and nothing at the same time. It asks you to accept the gap between values and practice as permanent. It suggests that wanting something different is a failure to understand reality. It offers belonging at the cost of silence.

You don't reject the culture outright. You work within it. You find small ways to soften its edges. You mentor newer responders quietly. You offer context when you can. You listen when others need to talk. These acts matter, even as you begin to feel the strain of holding both: participating in the culture and resisting its numbness.

This is how moral injury gets normalized—not through cruelty, but through repetition. Through phrases that smooth over discomfort instead of engaging it. Through cultures that prize continuity over coherence. Through good people doing their best inside systems that ask them to carry costs without naming them.

Most people don't leave because of this. They stay. They adjust. They call it realism, and in many ways, it is.

What they don't yet see is how much that realism is asking them to surrender.

What Gets Rewarded

You learn the rules without anyone ever teaching them to you. No one sits you down and explains what matters most here. There's no handbook for it. You absorb it the way you absorb everything else in disaster work: by watching what happens to people who act in certain ways.

You notice who gets praised. It isn't always the most compassionate responder or the one who asks the hardest questions. It's usually the person who keeps things moving, who solves problems quietly, who doesn't create friction. You see it early, even if you don't name it.

The first time you feel it directly is after a long shift. The site has been chaotic all day—lines backed up, tempers short, supplies slow to arrive. You spend most of your time de-escalating, translating decisions you didn't make into language people can tolerate. At the end of the day, leadership gathers the team briefly. Informal. Encouraging.

"Thanks for keeping things calm today," someone says, looking in your direction. "We really needed that."

It feels good to be seen. It also teaches you something: calm is currency.

Later, you notice how often calm is rewarded over clarity. Concerns framed as logistical problems get addressed faster than concerns framed as moral ones. Responders who ask fewer questions move more easily through the system. You start to understand the work values stability. In disasters, stability matters. Chaos helps no one. The problem isn't that stability is valued.

The problem is what gets sacrificed to preserve it.

You watch what happens when someone pushes too hard—not angrily, but persistently. They keep naming the same issue even after it's been acknowledged and set aside. They keep returning to impact, to harm, to what the decision means on the ground. People start avoiding them. Meetings move on without inviting their input. Conversations happen without them. They aren't punished, exactly.

They're just less included.

You learn from this. You don't stop caring.

You stop insisting.

Over time, you adjust. You raise concerns selectively. You soften language. You pick moments carefully. You accept compromises you would have challenged earlier, because you've learned which battles cost more than they change. This isn't moral collapse. It's adaptation. You're responding to incentives.

The organization doesn't ask you to betray your values outright. It asks you to prioritize—to decide which values are worth slowing things down for, and which ones need to wait. Indefinitely.

You notice how often efficiency gets framed as professionalism, how emotional restraint gets praised as maturity, how moral discomfort gets reframed as stress that can be managed individually. You hear things like: "Try not to take it personally." "You did what you could." "This is bigger than any one case." They're meant to help. They don't change the underlying conditions.

And you begin to see how silence gets reinforced—not through threats, but through relief. When a hard question isn't asked, the meeting runs smoother. When moral tension isn't named, the agenda stays on track. When no one challenges a decision, everyone can focus on what's next. Silence becomes efficient. Efficiency becomes virtue.

The clearest lesson comes when someone leaves. Not dramatically—quietly. They step away without much explanation. Maybe they take another role. Maybe they stop responding. People talk about it briefly. "They burned out." "It was too much for them." "They needed better boundaries." These explanations are tidy. They locate the problem in the individual. You rarely hear anyone ask what the work asked of them before they left.

As you advance, the rewards shift. You're trusted with more responsibility. You're invited into planning conversations. You're asked to mentor newer responders. It feels like progress. It is. It also puts you closer to decisions that will affect others in ways you cannot fully control. It adds pressure to model composure. People watch you. You become careful.

A newer responder comes to you after a difficult interaction. They aren't overwhelmed; they're troubled.

"I don't think that was okay," they say. "The way we handled that."

You listen. You agree. You also know what will happen if they push this further. You choose your words carefully.

"You're not wrong," you say. "But you have to pick your moments."

You watch their face as they absorb this, and you wonder whether you protected them or initiated them into the silence you've learned to navigate. This is how culture reproduces itself—not through policy, but through modeling. Through what gets rewarded, what gets ignored, and what quietly disappears. No one intends harm.

The harm still occurs.

You start to notice that praise often comes when you absorb cost without making it visible—when you smooth over a difficult interaction, prevent an issue from escalating, carry weight so others don't have to. You are good at this. The better you get, the more you are relied on. The more you are relied on, the less space there is to set the weight down.

At some point, you realize staying in good standing requires a certain kind of restraint—not dishonesty.

Containment.

You learn to hold moral discomfort internally while presenting calm externally. You learn to translate values into language that won't disrupt flow. You tell yourself this is leadership.

Sometimes it is.

Sometimes it's self-erasure.

What gets rewarded shapes who stays. People who can tolerate misalignment without naming it last longer. People who need coherence tend to leave, or go quiet, or step aside. No one says this out loud. They don't have to. The pattern speaks.

By now, you understand culture is not neutral. It shapes how the work is experienced, how cost is distributed, and who is allowed to name it. You are still committed. You still believe in the mission.

You also know something essential is being asked of you in return, and you're not sure how long that trade can hold.

When Silence Stops Working

Silence works until it doesn't. For a long time, it feels like the only responsible choice. You hold things in because naming them won't change the outcome, because the work must keep moving, because there isn't time to slow everything down for a conversation that won't fix the system. Silence feels mature—until one day it doesn't hold.

The moment is rarely dramatic. It isn't a confrontation or a breakdown. It's something small: a comment in passing, a decision stacked on top of another decision that never had time to settle. You're in the middle of a response that's gone on too long. Everyone is tired. Resources are thinner than expected. The same moral compromises you've been navigating for weeks are now routine.

Someone proposes a solution that will technically work. It will also push more burden onto responders already stretched thin. You feel the familiar tightening and wait, like you always do, for someone else to speak.

No one does.

You hear yourself say, "We can't keep doing this."

The room stills—not because you raised your voice, not because what you said is radical, but because you broke the rhythm. For a moment, no one responds. Then someone reframes it: short-term fixes, getting through this phase, revisiting concerns later. You nod. You know the script.

But something has shifted. You don't feel relief. You feel exposed.

Afterward, you replay it—not because you regret speaking, but because you realize how close you were to staying silent again, how long you've trained yourself to absorb strain without surfacing it. You notice your body's response—heat, adrenaline, the urge to retreat back into neutrality—and you also notice a strange clarity.

You said what was true.

That matters, even if nothing changes immediately.

The cracks in silence don't always appear in meetings. Sometimes they show up late at night, when the workday has officially ended but people are still there. Someone lingers after a shift and says, "Can I ask you something?" They don't ask about logistics. They ask how you keep doing this—not time management, but the moral weight. You hesitate. This isn't a conversation you're used to having openly. You answer carefully—honest, but not overwhelming—and watch their shoulders drop slightly.

They aren't alone.

That moment matters more than the meeting ever did.

You begin to notice these cracks more often. A colleague names frustration instead of covering it with humor. A supervisor acknowledges the toll of a decision instead of only its necessity. Someone says quietly, "That didn't sit right with me." No one proposes a solution. No policy changes. But something important has happened: the experience has been spoken.

Silence fails not because people become braver, but because the cost of holding it becomes heavier than the risk of breaking it. You see it in yourself. You're still careful. You still pick moments. But you no longer believe silence is neutral. You see how it redirects harm inward, where it accumulates quietly.

Culture doesn't change all at once. It shifts at the edges.

A newer responder challenges a decision in a way that would have once made you nervous—respectful, thoughtful, clear. You watch the room react. This time, you don't rush to smooth it over. You let the discomfort sit. It's uncomfortable.

It's also honest.

Later, the responder thanks you for not shutting the conversation down. You realize that sometimes the most meaningful intervention is restraint.

Not every crack leads to progress. Sometimes it leads to defensiveness, to fatigue, to people retreating again. You learn that naming moral strain doesn't guarantee repair.

It only creates the possibility of it.

That has to be enough.

The culture begins to feel less monolithic. You see pockets of difference—teams where people check in about more than logistics, leaders who admit uncertainty, responders who make space for grief without labeling it weakness. These moments are fragile, easy to lose when urgency returns. They require permission. They require attention.

You start thinking differently about leadership—not as authority, but as containment: the ability to hold moral complexity without forcing premature resolution, making room for truth even when it slows things down. This kind of leadership is rarely taught.

It's learned in the field.

By now, it's clear culture can either deepen moral injury or interrupt it—not through grand reforms, but through everyday choices. Through whether silence is rewarded or questioned. Through whether people are expected to absorb harm quietly or allowed to name it without penalty.

You don't pretend this will be fixed cleanly. But you no longer believe it's immutable. "This is just how it is" begins to lose its grip, not because reality changed, but because you've seen culture is made of people making choices, even constrained ones.

You leave this chapter without resolution. That's intentional. Culture doesn't transform cleanly.

But you now know this: silence is not the same as strength, and endurance is not the same as integrity. The work will always ask a lot.

The question is whether it also allows room for truth.

Chapter 5—How Responders Learn to Survive

The Habits That Keep You Going

You don't sit down one day and decide how you're going to survive this work. There's no moment of planning, no conscious choice between healthy and unhealthy strategies. You respond to what's in front of you with whatever tools are available at the time. The habits form quietly because the work keeps coming, and you need a way to stay upright inside it.

One of the first habits you develop is speed. Not rushing, exactly—momentum. You learn that staying in motion keeps certain feelings at bay. As long as there's another task, another person to check on, another form to complete, you don't have to linger anywhere too long. You get very good at it. When a conversation ends awkwardly, you pivot to the next one. When a decision leaves you unsettled, you document it and move on. When something doesn't sit right, you tell yourself you'll think about it later, even though later rarely comes.

People notice how efficient you are, how much you can hold, how you don't seem to get stuck. You take pride in that. It feels like competence.

Another habit is compartmentalization. You learn how to set parts of yourself aside when they're inconvenient. You don't shut them down completely; you put them somewhere they won't interfere. You tell yourself, I'll feel this later. Sometimes you do. Sometimes you don't. You become skilled at switching modes—work self, home self, public self, private self. The transitions get smoother over time, even as the distance between those selves grows. It helps, and it costs.

You notice how quickly you adapt your language. You stop using words that invite follow-up. You summarize instead of describing. You answer questions in ways that are accurate but contained: "How was today?" becomes "Busy." "What happened?" becomes "A lot." You aren't being evasive. You're being efficient. You've learned that telling the whole story often creates more work—emotional work, explanatory work—that you don't have the energy to manage—so you keep it brief.

Humor becomes another tool. Dark humor, dry humor, the kind that lives just this side of inappropriate. It doesn't show up around survivors; it shows up in back rooms, in cars, in late-night conversations with people who understand the context. You use it to release pressure, to signal belonging, to acknowledge absurdity without naming the harm directly. You're careful with it. You know when it crosses a line. Most of the time, it helps. Sometimes, you notice it creates distance. You laugh, and something closes off.

You also develop rules—personal ones. Rules about how attached you'll let yourself get. About how much time you'll spend thinking about cases once they're closed. About which battles you'll fight and which ones you won't. You tell yourself these rules are about boundaries. They are. They're also about survival. You've learned, often the hard way, that total openness isn't sustainable. You've seen people try to stay fully porous, fully engaged, fully affected.

They don't last.

So you adjust.

One of the most subtle habits is how you manage hope. Early on, you're generous with it. You imagine better outcomes. You believe effort will usually lead somewhere meaningful. You let yourself picture things improving. Over time, hope becomes something you ration—not because you've become cynical, but because you've learned that unguarded hope can hurt. You still care deeply; you just temper expectation. You tell yourself this is realism, and it is, but it also changes how the work feels.

There's a moment when you realize that many of the habits keeping you functional were never designed to help you heal. They help you stay. They help you perform. They help you get through the day. They don't necessarily help you integrate what the day has asked of you. You don't always notice this consciously. You just notice that certain feelings don't resolve anymore. They fade, or flatten, or resurface later without context. You accept this as the cost of doing the work.

You see these habits mirrored in others: the responder who never stops moving, the colleague who jokes through the hardest parts, the supervisor who is endlessly calm but hard to read. You recognize the patterns because you share them. There's comfort in that, and there's a quiet question forming underneath.

You don't think of these strategies as coping mechanisms. They don't feel therapeutic or intentional. They feel like common sense, like professionalism, like maturity earned through experience—and many of them are exactly that. The problem isn't that they exist. The problem is that they're often the only tools available.

At some point, you notice that rest alone doesn't undo the impact of these habits. You take time off. You sleep. You disconnect. Some things improve. Others don't. The speed comes back quickly. The compartmentalization snaps into place the moment you return. The humor resumes. The rules reassert themselves. It's efficient. It's familiar.

It's not quite enough.

You aren't failing at self-care. You're surviving in a system that rewards certain adaptations and offers few alternatives. That distinction matters, because without it you're likely to blame yourself for strategies that were never meant to do more than keep you functioning. This chapter isn't here to judge these habits. They developed for a reason. They allowed you to keep showing up. They may still be doing that.

But as the work continues, a question begins to surface, quietly and insistently: Are the habits that helped me survive still helping me stay whole? You don't answer that question yet. You just notice it's there.

When the Strategies Start to Cost More Than They Give

You become known for your calm. Not officially. No one announces it. It's just something people start to say, usually with relief. When things get tense, someone looks around and says, "Can you handle this?" And more often than not, they mean you.

You don't mind. You've worked hard for that steadiness. You know how to lower your voice when others raise theirs. You know how to slow your breathing when a room gets charged. You know how to absorb anger without reacting. It feels like competence. It feels like control.

During one response, the role becomes explicit. A supervisor pulls you aside early in the day. "If anything gets heated," they say, "I want you on it." You nod. Of course.

The site is crowded. Wait times are long. Information keeps changing. You move from one tense interaction to another—de-escalating, explaining, translating disappointment into something survivable. You do it well. People comment on it.

"You're so steady," someone says.

"I don't know how you stay so calm," says another.

You smile. You shrug it off. Inside, you feel a familiar tightening, but you keep going.

Late in the afternoon, a younger responder asks if they can shadow you for a bit. They've had a rough interaction and want to see how you handle things. You agree. The next conversation is with a man who's been waiting for hours. He's frustrated, bordering on angry. You step in smoothly, take over the exchange, lower the temperature in the room within minutes. You explain the limits clearly. You acknowledge frustration without validating anger. You redirect toward what can be done.

It works. The man leaves calmer than he arrived.

The younger responder watches closely. Afterward, they say, "I wish I could do that. You didn't even seem affected." The comment lands strangely. You hadn't noticed until then how little you were letting yourself feel.

As the day goes on, you stay in that mode—steady, contained, unflappable. You notice people start routing the hardest interactions to you automatically. You don't object. It's easier than pushing back. It keeps things from escalating. By the end of the shift, you're exhausted in a way that feels different from physical tiredness, and you don't mention it.

At the end-of-day check-in, leadership thanks the team and singles you out again. "Really appreciate how you handled things today," they say. "You kept everything from boiling over." Everyone nods. You nod too.

That night, at home, the quiet feels louder than usual. You sit down and realize you don't remember much about the conversations themselves. You remember the mechanics—the phrases, the sequence, the way each interaction was managed. You don't remember what you felt. That's when you notice something else: no one checked in with you. Not because they don't care, but because you didn't look like you needed it.

A few days later, you run into the younger responder again. They mention the interaction you handled and say they tried to do something similar afterward. "It didn't really work," they admit. "The person just shut down." You think about that and realize what they saw wasn't the internal work it took to stay present without hardening. They saw the exterior result, not the cost. You didn't teach them how to do it.

You taught them how to look like it didn't matter.

That realization stays with you longer than you expect. By the time you reach the next response, you notice how easily the role snaps back into place—the calm, the containment, the steady presence everyone relies on. It still works.

It just costs more than it used to.

And you're not sure how long you can afford it.

You don't notice the shift right away. That's part of what makes it hard to name. The habits you've developed are still working, at least on the surface. You're showing up. You're functioning. You're meeting expectations. Nothing has fallen apart. From the outside, it looks like resilience. From the inside, something feels thinner.

The first thing you notice is how quickly you move past moments that once would have stayed with you. Not because they don't matter, but because you don't have the capacity to hold them the way you used to. You listen, respond, do what's required, and then you move on. You tell yourself this is efficiency. It is. It's also compression—you're packing more experience into less internal space.

Speed, which once protected you, begins to flatten things. You finish one conversation and immediately start another. You resolve one issue and move on to the next without pause. There's no space between moments for meaning to settle. At first, this feels like mastery. Later, it feels like drift. You can go through an entire day without really registering what happened in it. You remember the tasks, the sequence, the outcomes. You struggle to remember how it felt.

Compartmentalization begins to leak. You still tell yourself you'll feel things later, but later doesn't always come—or when it does, it arrives out of context. A small frustration at home triggers an outsized reaction. A minor inconvenience feels heavier than it should. You're surprised by your own intensity, or by your lack of it. You wonder when you started carrying work residue into places you once protected from it.

Humor changes too. It's still sharp, still shared, still useful in certain moments. But you notice it sometimes lands differently now. A joke that once released tension now closes something off. A laugh comes more easily than a sigh. You reach for wit before vulnerability, even when vulnerability would be more honest. You don't become cruel. You become defended.

The rules you made to protect yourself begin to harden. You notice how quickly you disengage from cases that feel too complex. You find yourself categorizing people earlier, narrowing your emotional investment before you fully understand the situation. You tell yourself this is boundary-setting. It is. It's also avoidance—not of work, but of the moral weight the work carries.

Hope is where the cost becomes clearest. You still believe in the mission. You still care deeply about the people you serve. But you stop letting yourself imagine outcomes that feel just. You aim lower—not because you don't want better, but because disappointment hurts more than resignation. You stop expecting alignment. You stop being surprised by harm. This protects you.

It also dulls something essential.

None of this feels dramatic. You aren't spiraling or breaking down. You're adapting. The problem is that adaptation isn't neutral. It reshapes you. You begin to notice how often your internal responses are shaped by prediction rather than presence. You anticipate where a conversation is going and emotionally check out before it gets there. You preemptively soften expectations to avoid being unsettled. You are still attentive.

You are less open.

There's a moment when you catch yourself thinking, I don't want to hear this again. Not about a person—about a situation, a familiar pattern of need meeting constraint. The thought shocks you. You don't say it. You don't even fully believe it. But it's there, and it tells you something important.

You start to feel tired in a way that rest doesn't resolve. Sleep helps your body. Time off helps your schedule. Neither touches the sense of moral saturation you're carrying. You've been absorbing misalignment for a long time, and it has nowhere to go.

You may notice a subtle narrowing in how you see yourself. You identify more with your role than with your values. You talk about what you do more than why you do it. You rely on competence to anchor your sense of worth. This works—until it doesn't.

None of this means your survival strategies were wrong. They were necessary. They allowed you to stay when staying mattered. But strategies that help you survive a season can cost you if they become permanent. That isn't a personal failure. It's a predictable outcome.

You begin to sense that something needs to change, even if you don't know what. You can't simply drop the habits. They're ingrained, functional, reinforced by the culture around you. You also can't ignore the cost anymore. The gap between survival and sustainability has become visible.

This realization doesn't come with instructions.

It comes with a question: What would it mean to stay in this work without having to shrink? You don't answer it yet. You just let it sit.

Testing What Might Help You Stay Whole

You don't overhaul your life. That's not how change happens in this work. You don't suddenly abandon the habits that kept you afloat. You don't announce a new philosophy. You don't step away from responsibility. What you do instead is experiment—carefully, almost privately.

The first experiment is slowing down, just slightly. Not enough to disrupt operations or draw attention. Just enough to notice what happens if you don't immediately move on from a moment that unsettles you. You stay with a conversation for an extra beat. You take a breath before transitioning. You allow yourself to feel the discomfort instead of filing it away. It feels inefficient.

It also feels honest.

When you slow down like this, certain things surface—not overwhelm, not collapse.

Clarity.

You realize how often you've been outrunning your own reactions, how much effort that took, how much quieter things feel when you stop doing it for a moment. You don't do this all the time. You couldn't. But you do it enough to learn something.

Another experiment is choosing who you speak honestly with. Not everyone. Not publicly. One or two people who understand the work well enough not to need explanation—people who don't rush to fix or minimize, people who can sit with complexity without needing resolution. You test the water. You say something you usually wouldn't.

"That one didn't sit right with me."
"I'm having trouble letting that go."
"I feel conflicted about what we did."

You wait. The response matters. When the response is rushed or dismissive, you pull back. When it's patient, you feel something loosen. You realize how rare that kind of listening has become.

You begin to pay attention to language—not in a self-monitoring way, but in a noticing way. You catch yourself when you default to phrases that flatten experience. You experiment with saying one sentence more than you normally would—not a full story, just enough to let the truth breathe. You notice how often people respond with relief.

They were carrying something similar.

You also start to differentiate between boundaries that protect you and boundaries that isolate you. This takes time. You notice which rules keep you from being overwhelmed and which ones keep you from being affected at all. You don't remove the boundaries. You soften a few. You allow yourself to care in places where you had gone numb. It's risky.

It's also enlivening.

There's an experiment that feels almost subversive: you stop trying to make every moral tension disappear. Instead of immediately explaining or justifying a difficult decision, you sometimes name the tension itself. "This is hard." "I wish this were different." "I don't feel great about this either." You don't say these things to everyone. You say them when it's safe. You notice how often they change the interaction—not the outcome.

The tone.

That matters more than you expected.

You begin to understand that sustainability doesn't come from eliminating moral strain. It comes from not carrying it alone. This is a shift. You've been trained to be strong, composed, to hold things together. You begin to see that wholeness sometimes requires shared weight, not greater strength.

You also experiment with how you leave the work each day. Not dramatically. You don't debrief every moment. You simply mark the transition. You name, quietly, what stayed with you. You resist the urge to numb immediately. You allow the residue to be acknowledged rather than managed away.

This doesn't make the work lighter.

It makes it less diffuse.

Over time, these small experiments change something—not the system.

You.

You feel more present even when the work is hard. You notice less internal fragmentation. You feel less like you're splitting yourself to stay functional. You are still tired.

You are less hollow.

You don't pretend this is a solution. There are days when none of this helps—days when constraints are too tight, misalignment too stark. You don't romanticize the work. You stay realistic. But you no longer confuse survival with sustainability.

You begin to see that staying whole is not about perfect balance.

It's about ongoing repair.

This chapter isn't offering a checklist. There is no program here. What it offers is permission: permission to notice which habits serve you now and which ones may have outlived their usefulness; permission to experiment without announcing; permission to value integrity as much as endurance.

You don't have to decide everything at once. You just have to stop assuming that the only way to stay is to shrink.

That assumption has cost too much already.

Chapter 6—**When Survival Stops Being Enough**

The Moment the Old Tools Fail

For a long time, survival felt sufficient. You weren't thriving exactly, but you were steady. You showed up. You did the work. You used the habits you'd developed to stay functional, and for a while they worked well enough that you didn't question them—until one day they didn't.

It doesn't happen during a crisis. It happens in the quiet stretch afterward, when things are supposed to be easier—when urgency lifts just enough for you to notice what's underneath. You're on a response that's winding down. The pace has slowed. The site is smaller now. Fewer people, fewer fires to put out. This is usually when relief shows up. Instead, you feel flat. Not exhausted in the way you recognize, not overwhelmed—just empty of the satisfaction you expected when things finally eased. You tell yourself it's normal, a letdown after intensity. You've felt it before.

This feels different.

You're sitting with a survivor who's come back for a follow-up conversation. You've already explained what's possible. You've already given referrals. This is more about reassurance than action.

They talk. You listen. You say the right things. You're attentive. You're calm. From the outside, nothing is missing. From the inside, you feel oddly detached, relying almost entirely on technique now: the phrases, the pacing, the practiced empathy that once felt like an extension of who you were and now feels more like a tool you pick up when needed.

It still works, and that's what scares you.

After the conversation ends, you sit alone for a moment and realize you don't feel anything about it. No sadness, no frustration, no connection—just completion. You finish the task and move on. This should feel like efficiency. Instead, it feels like loss.

You begin to notice how often you're operating this way. You move from interaction to interaction with competence but little resonance. You handle difficult conversations smoothly, but they don't stay with you the way they once did. At first, you're grateful. This is what I wanted, you think. Less impact. Less weight. Then you realize something else has gone quiet too: the moments that used to sustain you. The brief connections. The sense of meaning that made the cost feel worth it. They're harder to find.

One evening, a newer responder asks how you manage to keep going. They're asking sincerely. They admire your steadiness. They want to learn from you. You pause. You used to answer easily—purpose, calling, presence. This time, the words don't come. Not because you don't believe them, but because they don't feel complete anymore. You offer something practical instead: pacing, boundaries, don't take it home. They thank you, and you feel like you've handed them a map that no longer includes the terrain you're standing on.

The old tools haven't disappeared. You still compartmentalize. You still move quickly when needed. You still use humor to release pressure. You still manage expectations carefully. These strategies haven't failed outright; they've just stopped being enough. They keep you functioning. They don't help you feel intact.

You notice the shift most clearly when something genuinely good happens: a family gets what they need, a resource comes through unexpectedly, a situation resolves better than you anticipated. You register it intellectually. You even smile. But the lift doesn't last. It doesn't sink in. You move on as quickly as you would have moved on from disappointment. That's when you realize the issue isn't just numbness to pain. It's numbness to meaning.

This realization is unsettling. You didn't come into this work to feel nothing. You accepted that it would hurt sometimes. You accepted strain, limits, moral tension. What you didn't expect was this quiet erosion of significance. You begin to understand that survival strategies can flatten the entire emotional landscape if they're used too long without repair. They don't discriminate between what hurts and what matters.

You don't talk about this easily. It sounds ungrateful, or dramatic, or like complaining about something you should simply accept as the price of longevity. So you keep it to yourself. You tell yourself you're lucky to still be here, lucky to still be capable, lucky to still care as much as you do—and you do care. That's the problem.

You realize survival is a short-term goal that has quietly become a long-term plan. Survival is about getting through. Staying is about something else entirely.

There's a moment, later than you expect, when this becomes undeniable. You're explaining the work to someone outside the field. They ask why you keep doing it. You start with the usual answers, then you stop. You hear how thin they sound. You realize you're describing the work accurately, but not honestly—you're describing what you do, not what it costs, not what it used to give you. That's when it becomes clear something needs attention. Not a break. Not a new strategy layered on top of the old ones. Something deeper.

You don't know what that is yet. You only know that staying alive in the work is no longer enough. You want to stay present. You want the work to mean something again. You want your values to feel engaged, not just managed.

This is the moment many responders reach quietly. They don't announce it or label it. They simply recognize that endurance without meaning is a kind of loss they can't afford indefinitely. They haven't given up. They aren't leaving. They're standing at a threshold, whether they know it or not. Survival got them here. Something else will be required to keep them whole.

Trying to Fix the Wrong Thing

When you first realize survival isn't enough anymore, your instinct is to fix it the same way you've fixed everything else. You look for an adjustment—something you can add or remove, a lever you can pull that will restore what's gone missing without asking too much of you or the system.

You start with the obvious places. You take a longer break between responses. You turn down an assignment you would have accepted automatically a year ago. You tell yourself this is wisdom, not withdrawal. You've earned the right to pace yourself.

The time off is good. You sleep. You catch up on small things you've been postponing. You spend time with people who know you outside the work. Your body feels better. The constant low-level alertness eases. You think, This was it. I just needed space. When the next response comes, you feel ready.

You arrive rested, grounded, clear. The site is familiar. The rhythm comes back quickly. You step into your role with the same competence you've always had—maybe even a little more patience than usual. At first, it feels better. You're less reactive. You don't feel as rushed. You notice tension rising and address it early. You tell yourself this is what sustainability looks like.

Then, somewhere in the middle of the day, the same hollowness appears. Not sharply—just unmistakably. It happens during a conversation that should matter to you. A survivor is explaining their situation. It's complicated, layered. You listen carefully. You respond appropriately. You offer what's available. You do everything you're supposed to do, and you notice with strange clarity that you're not fully there. You're present, but distant. Engaged, but insulated. You finish the conversation and move on, unsettled.

You had rested for this.

After that response, you make another adjustment. You shift your role slightly—less direct service, more coordination, more planning. Fewer one-on-one interactions where expectations and limits collide. It seems like a smart move. You're still contributing, still valued, still useful. The work feels lighter.

And thinner.

You miss the immediacy of the field even as you remember why it became hard. You find yourself longing for moments of connection while also guarding against their cost. You didn't expect to miss what wore you down.

You try training next. Trauma-informed care. Resilience. Compassion fatigue. The language is familiar. The facilitators are skilled. You nod along. Some of it resonates. Some of it feels adjacent. You practice grounding techniques. You refine transitions. You get better at noticing when you're overloaded. You apply what you've learned.

It helps with stress.

It doesn't touch the emptiness.

People around you think you're doing better. You look more rested. You sound more measured. You're saying no when you need to. You're modeling all the things people talk about when they talk about sustainability. You start receiving comments: "I'm glad you're taking care of yourself." "You seem more balanced." "This is what longevity looks like." You nod. You want to believe them.

One afternoon, you're asked to step into a difficult situation because you're known for handling them well. You agree. You walk into the conversation calm and prepared. You explain the decision clearly. You manage the emotions in the room. You de-escalate without minimizing. You do everything right. When it's over, someone thanks you.

"Handled perfectly," they say.

You walk away feeling nothing. Not relief. Not pride. Just completion. That's when you realize something important: competence has remained intact. Meaning has not.

That evening, you try to make sense of it. You review everything you've changed—more rest, better boundaries, fewer exposures, new skills, more intentional pacing. All of it is reasonable. All of it is responsible. None of it has addressed what's actually missing. You haven't been overextended.

You've been misaligned.

The realization doesn't come with clarity about what to do next. It comes with frustration. You've done what the culture tells you to do when the work gets hard. You've followed the advice you've given others. You've invested in yourself. And still, something essential feels absent.

You begin to understand why some people describe this phase as dangerous—not because it leads to collapse, but because it leads to quiet disillusionment. You don't want to leave. That's not the conclusion you're drawing. You want the work to feel real again. You want to feel engaged rather than managed. You want to recognize yourself in the role, not just perform it well.

This is the moment when it becomes clear you've been trying to solve the wrong problem. You thought the issue was depletion. It wasn't. You thought the solution was rest. It helped, but it wasn't enough. What's missing isn't energy.

It's moral contact.

You don't have that language yet. You just know this: if survival requires you to keep adjusting yourself while the moral strain remains untouched, something is being asked of you that no amount of self-management can satisfy. And for the first time, you stop looking for another fix.

When Something Finally Helps

The first thing that helps doesn't look like a solution. It doesn't arrive as a program or a training or a clearly defined practice. It isn't something you sign up for or schedule in advance. If someone had described it to you beforehand, you might have dismissed it as insufficient. It shows up quietly, almost accidentally.

You're on a response that feels familiar in all the ways that usually concern you. The constraints are there. The decisions are imperfect. The limits are clear. You recognize the moral pressure points as soon as you arrive. You brace yourself for the familiar flattening.

Instead, something small interrupts the pattern.

A colleague asks how you're doing—not in the reflexive way people ask in passing, but with enough pause afterward that you realize they're actually waiting for an answer. You almost give the standard one. Then you don't.

"I'm having a harder time with this than I expected," you say.

You don't elaborate. You don't explain. You let the sentence stand. They nod. "Yeah," they say. "Me too." That's it. No fixing. No reframing. No reassurance that it will all be okay.

Just recognition.

Something in you settles.

You notice afterward that the work feels slightly different. Not easier—less lonely. You're still operating within the same constraints. You still say no when you have to. You still carry decisions you wish were different. But now, when something doesn't sit right, you know there is at least one place where that discomfort can land. That matters more than you expected.

The next moment comes later. You're enforcing a decision you don't fully agree with. You explain it carefully. You watch disappointment register. Normally you'd move quickly, contain the interaction, manage the fallout internally.

This time, you pause.

"I wish this were different," you say quietly.

The person looks at you. You don't justify it. You don't walk it back. You don't promise what you can't deliver. You name the truth. They nod slowly. "I know," they say. The outcome doesn't change. The interaction does.

You start to notice that moments like this don't reduce your professionalism. They deepen it. They allow you to stay aligned without pretending alignment exists where it doesn't. They let you stay present without hardening. You realize repair doesn't always mean relief.

Sometimes it means coherence.

Another moment comes outside the field. You're talking with someone who understands the work well enough not to be alarmed by its complexity. You describe a situation that's been bothering you—not in full detail, just enough to convey the moral tension. They don't interrupt. They don't rush to empathize. They say, "That sounds like it put you in an impossible position." You hadn't used that phrase. It lands with precision. You feel the familiar recognition again, but this time it isn't isolating.

It's shared.

You begin to see a pattern. What helps isn't escape from moral strain.

It's contact around it.

Moments where the moral reality of the work is acknowledged rather than smoothed over. Where the cost is named without being exaggerated or minimized. Where you're allowed to say, "This matters," even when nothing can be fixed. You realize how rarely that happens, and how powerful it is when it does.

You experiment, cautiously, with allowing these moments. You don't force them. You don't demand them from people who can't offer them. You simply stop shutting them down when they appear. You let a conversation linger when it wants to. You resist the urge to translate everything into action steps. You let someone else's discomfort exist without immediately absorbing it or deflecting it.

It feels risky.

It also feels grounding.

Over time, these moments begin to stitch something back together—not all at once, not completely, but enough that you no longer feel like you're constantly splitting yourself to stay functional. You notice meaning hasn't disappeared.

It's been buried under strategies that kept you alive but left little room for truth.

As space opens, meaning returns in fragments. That's enough.

You stop looking for a fix. You start paying attention to repair. Repair looks like honesty without collapse, connection without performance, staying in the work without pretending it's harmless. Repair doesn't eliminate moral injury. It interrupts its isolation.

By the end of this chapter, nothing is resolved in the way you once hoped it might be. Systems are still constrained. Decisions are still imperfect. The work still asks too much at times. What's changed is this: you no longer believe survival has to come at the cost of integrity. You've seen that meaning can be restored not by doing more, but by letting the truth of the work be spoken and shared.

That knowledge doesn't make the work lighter.

It makes it possible to keep going without disappearing inside it.

Chapter 7—**The Weight of Repetition**

It Adds Up

The first few times, you tell yourself each response stands alone. This one has its own circumstances, its own people, its own limits. When it ends, you close it the way you were taught to close things, and you move on.

For a while, that works. Then one day you realize you aren't starting from zero anymore.

You notice it at the beginning of a response that feels familiar in ways you don't have time to examine. The briefing sounds like other briefings. The site setup follows patterns you've memorized. The language people use to describe the situation is the same language you've heard dozens of times. You know what's coming—not the specifics, but the shape. You know where the bottlenecks will form. You know which questions will go unanswered. You know the moment when expectations will collide with reality and someone will look to you to explain why.

You haven't even arrived at the site yet, and your body is already preparing.

Early in the response, someone thanks you for being there. They say it with sincerity, gratitude sharpened by exhaustion. You nod. You appreciate it. You also feel something else: the awareness that this isn't the first time you've heard those words, and it won't be the last. Gratitude matters, but it doesn't counterbalance the accumulation of what the work has been asking of you over time. It never could.

Repetition shows up most clearly in moments that mirror each other across years: a conversation you've had before with different names, a decision you've enforced before with a different justification, a disappointment that lands the same way it always does. You recognize the emotional arc as it unfolds. You know when frustration will turn into resignation. You know when someone will stop asking questions. You know when it's time to shift from explanation to containment.

You perform the role expertly. You've learned how to do this. At first, you're grateful for that expertise. It smooths the work. It reduces chaos. It protects people from unnecessary harm. Experience matters.

The problem isn't competence. The problem is what competence begins to carry over time.

You begin to feel the weight of unresolved endings. So few responses end cleanly. So many stories stop mid-sentence. People leave without resolution. Needs remain unmet. Decisions linger without repair. At the end of each response, you pack up and move on, but something stays behind in you. You don't consciously collect these moments.

They collect you.

The accumulation isn't dramatic. It doesn't announce itself as trauma. It shows up as familiarity that has lost its neutrality: a phrase that triggers you before you've thought about it, a situation that feels heavy the moment it appears because you know how it usually ends. You aren't pessimistic.

You're remembering.

There's a moment in this response that mirrors one from years ago. Someone sits across from you and asks the same question you've been asked dozens of times. They're polite, hopeful, trying to understand how this could have happened to them. You hear yourself answering with words you've refined over time. As you speak, you realize you could deliver this explanation in your sleep, and that realization lands harder than the content of the conversation.

Afterward, you feel a flicker of grief—not for this person alone, but for all the people who came before them. For the fact that the system hasn't learned what you have learned. For the way you've had to absorb that knowledge quietly, without any mechanism for release or resolution. You don't say this to anyone. There isn't time.

You begin to see how repetition compounds moral strain. Each individual response may be manageable. Each decision defensible. Each compromise understandable. Taken together, they form a pattern that presses against your values again and again—never quite enough to break them, but enough to bend them.

You notice you're carrying a sense of inevitability now. Not about disaster.

About response.

You know how this will go. That knowledge doesn't make you less committed. It makes you more tired.

A newer responder reacts strongly to a situation you've seen many times. They name the injustice plainly. They ask why this keeps happening. You listen and remember feeling that way, and then you realize you don't feel it the same way anymore. That realization unsettles you—not because you think you've stopped caring, but because you can feel how much you've absorbed to keep going.

You reassure them. You offer context. You explain constraints. You help them understand the system. You hear yourself saying things that once frustrated you when others said them. You recognize the shift. You aren't proud of it. You aren't ashamed either.

You're aware.

This is how repetition works. It doesn't numb you all at once. It trains you. It teaches you what to expect, what to tolerate, what not to be surprised by. It also quietly recalibrates your moral center, asking it to accommodate more than it was ever meant to hold.

At the end of the day, you review your notes. The facts are accurate. The outcomes documented. The work complete. You sit for a moment longer than necessary and feel the accumulation—not as a single weight, but as a layered one. You realize then that moral injury isn't only about singular moments of violation. It's about repetition without repair, about carrying unresolved moral tension again and again until it becomes part of the background of your life.

You're still capable. Still committed.

But you're no longer untouched.

This chapter isn't about burnout. It's about accrual—what happens when the work keeps asking the same hard things and offers no meaningful resolution. By the end of this part you don't feel alarmed.

You feel informed.

You understand something you didn't before: it isn't just what you've seen.

It's how often you've been asked to see it.

Who You Become Over Time

Repetition doesn't just change how the work feels. It changes how you understand yourself inside it.

At first, the shift is subtle. You don't wake up one day feeling like a different person. You wake up knowing exactly who you are in these environments, and that's the problem. You become the steady one—the experienced one, the person others look to when things stall or emotions rise. You know how to move conversations forward. You know how to say no without sounding cruel. You know how to keep the work from unraveling when pressure builds.

This identity is earned, and it's reinforced constantly. People trust you. Supervisors rely on you. Newer responders watch you, trying to learn how you manage what they're still struggling to hold. You carry that responsibility seriously.

Over time, you notice the role has begun to narrow how you're allowed to show up. Not officially. No one tells you to feel less. No one asks you to silence your values outright. But there's an unspoken understanding that certain reactions don't fit the version of you people have come to depend on. You're expected to be composed, measured, reliable. You live up to that expectation, even when it means setting parts of yourself aside.

You begin to see how repetition shapes credibility. Early on, you asked questions freely. You expressed uncertainty. You named discomfort as it arose. You hadn't yet learned which reactions were considered productive and which ones created friction.

Now you know. You know how to phrase things so they're taken seriously. You know when to push and when to hold back. You know how to present concerns without being dismissed as emotional or impractical.

This is skill.

It's also constraint.

Your internal reactions shift too. You still recognize moral tension. You still see injustice when it appears. But the intensity is different. The edges are softer. The response more muted. At first, you tell yourself this is growth—perspective. You've learned not to react to everything as if it's new.

That's true. It's also incomplete.

A decision is made quickly. A comment minimizes impact. A policy is applied without nuance. You feel the familiar flicker of discomfort, and you also feel how quickly your body moves to contain it. You don't linger. You don't question out loud. You move on, telling yourself you'll revisit it later if needed.

Later rarely comes.

Repetition teaches you which reactions are safe to have and which ones are better managed internally. You don't become indifferent. You become selective. You conserve emotional energy the way you conserve physical energy, because you've learned what happens when you don't. This makes you effective.

It also makes you quieter.

Outside the work, the shift becomes more visible. Friends describe you as grounded, calm, unflappable—someone who's "seen a lot" and doesn't get worked up easily. You recognize the truth in that. You also notice how rarely you talk about what still moves you, what still unsettles you, what still feels unresolved. It isn't that those things don't exist.

They've just learned to stay inside.

You begin to identify more with the role than with the values that drew you to it. Not because you've abandoned those values, but because the role demands consistency in ways values don't always accommodate. You become fluent in the language of response: acronyms, frameworks, decision trees. You can explain why things happen the way they do, and sometimes you catch yourself using those explanations to quiet your own unease.

A newer responder pushes back hard against a decision. They name the moral problem directly. They ask why the system keeps functioning this way. You listen and remember asking the same questions. Then you hear yourself responding with context, not conviction—constraints, perspective, patience. You see the shift happen in them as you speak. Not agreement.

Adjustment.

You wonder whether you helped them, or moved them one step closer to the same accommodation you've made.

This is one of the quieter costs of repetition. It doesn't just wear you down. It reshapes you into someone who can carry the work without disruption. That adaptation is rewarded.

It is also absorbing.

You don't lose your sense of right and wrong. You lose the expectation that right and wrong will be resolved. You adjust to living with the gap. You stop expecting coherence. You stop being surprised by misalignment. This makes the work survivable.

It also makes it harder to imagine anything else.

At some point you realize the question isn't whether repetition has changed you. It has. The question is whether the change has been intentional—whether you've had any say in who you're becoming, or whether repetition has been shaping you by default. That question doesn't have an easy answer.

It lingers.

You are still committed. Still capable. Still trusted. You are also carrying an identity formed under repeated moral strain, without much opportunity for reflection or repair. That matters, because identity shapes not just how you work, but what you tolerate, what you believe you deserve, and what you imagine is possible.

By the end of this part, you haven't reached a conclusion.

You've reached clarity.

Repetition doesn't just accumulate experiences.

It accumulates selves.

And if that process goes unnamed, it will keep shaping you long after you stop noticing it.

When the Accumulation Reaches a Limit

This response goes well. That's the first thing you notice.

Coordination is smooth. Information is clear. The team is staffed adequately for once. The site opens on time. People move through the process without major disruption. By every external measure, this is a good operation. You know how rare that is, and you step into the day with confidence. You know the layout and the flow. You know where problems usually surface and how to intercept them early. You're effective. People defer to you without hesitation. When a question comes up, someone says, "Ask him," and points in your direction. You answer quickly, decisively.

The work moves.

Midway through the morning, you're pulled into a situation that looks exactly like dozens you've handled before. Someone has been waiting longer than expected. They aren't angry yet, but they're close. They want to know why the process is taking so long and whether it's even worth staying. You approach calmly. You introduce yourself. You listen. They explain their situation carefully, trying not to lose control. You nod. You understand immediately where this is headed.

You've walked this path many times.

You explain the delay. You name the constraints. You offer what reassurance you can without promising what you can't deliver. You do it well. You always do. As you're speaking, you realize you aren't improvising at all. Every sentence is familiar. Every pause deliberate. Every word refined through repetition.

You could say this in your sleep, and that realization lands in your body before it reaches your mind.

They listen. They nod. They accept the explanation, even if they don't like it. "Okay," they say finally. "I guess we'll wait." You thank them. You move on. From the outside, the interaction couldn't have gone better. Inside, you feel something tighten—just enough to notice. You don't feel relief. You don't feel satisfaction.

You feel completion.

And beneath it, a weariness that doesn't belong to this single exchange.

Later a colleague comments on how smoothly things are going. "This is one of the better ones," they say. You agree—and realize the sentence has stopped meaning what it used to mean. A better response still ends with unmet needs. It still requires you to absorb disappointment and present it calmly, repeatedly, as if it were new. Efficiency hasn't changed that.

In the afternoon you overhear a newer responder talking quietly. "I don't know how you all do this over and over," they say. "It's exhausting." You almost laugh. Not because he's wrong, but because he's right in a way he doesn't yet understand. You think back over your years in this work—not response by response, but pattern by pattern. The same conversations. The same explanations. The same careful balancing of honesty and hope. The same endings that aren't really endings. You realize you've been carrying all of them into each new response.

They haven't stayed separate.

They've layered.

Near the end of the day you're asked to step into another situation. Someone wants an exception. Policy doesn't allow it. You know immediately. You've seen this exact scenario play out before. You explain the policy. They push back. You explain again. They stop arguing, not because they agree, but because they're tired. You recognize the moment when hope collapses into resignation.

You've witnessed it too many times to count.

When the interaction ends, you feel something close to grief—accumulated grief. You feel it for this person and for all the others who left like this, quietly, carrying disappointment without spectacle. You feel it for yourself, for how practiced you've become at delivering this outcome.

You step outside for a moment. The air feels different when you pause long enough to notice it. You watch people move in and out of the building, each carrying their own version of the day.

Nothing about this response has gone wrong.

That's the problem.

This is when it becomes clear—not in a flash, but in a settling. The weight isn't about any single response being too much. It's about how many times you've been asked to be the steady point in the same moral pattern, without resolution. You've been reliable. You've been effective. You've been present.

And you've been absorbing something no one ever asked whether you could keep carrying.

You don't feel angry. You don't feel ready to leave. You feel aware—aware that repetition has crossed from experience into burden, that competence has masked accumulation, that doing this well hasn't protected you from its cost. You go back inside and finish the day. You do your job. You do it as well as you always have.

But now you can't pretend this is just another response.

You know something has reached its limit.

Not in the work.

In you.

There is no single moment when repetition becomes too much. If there were, it would be easier to manage, easier to explain, easier to justify. Instead, the limit announces itself indirectly, through signals that are easy to misread. You don't think, I can't do this anymore. You think, Something has shifted.

A request comes in that mirrors dozens you've handled before. You know the steps. You know the likely outcome. You also feel a heaviness that doesn't match the task in front of you. You pause longer than necessary, and you notice the pause.

That's new.

The work hasn't gotten harder in any obvious way. In fact, you're better at it than ever. You anticipate problems early. You intervene smoothly. You make fewer mistakes. People rely on you more, not less. That's what makes this confusing. If the work is going well, why does it feel heavier?

Sometimes the limit shows up as irritation that feels out of proportion—not explosive, just sharper than you expect. You're surprised by how quickly you feel tired of explaining the same things again, how little patience you have for systems you understand deeply and still find ethically thin. You don't act on it. You register it and wonder where it came from.

Other times the signal is emotional blunting. You hear stories that would have once stayed with you, and you notice they don't linger in the same way. You feel concern, but not connection. Sadness, but not resonance. You tell yourself this is professionalism. You've learned not to take everything home.

Still, you miss the feeling of being moved.

You might notice the limit at home. Someone asks how work is going and you feel resistance rise up—not because you don't want to talk, but because you don't know how to summarize years of accumulation in a sentence or two. You give a neutral answer. You change the subject. Later you feel a distance that wasn't there before.

It can show up physically too: tightness in your chest during meetings, heaviness at the start of responses, fatigue that doesn't lift with rest. You check the usual boxes—sleep, nutrition, exercise, time off. Nothing is wrong enough to diagnose.

Something is still off.

At some point you realize you aren't just carrying the current response. You're carrying all the ones before it: unresolved endings, compromises that made sense in the moment but never sat right, the ways you adjusted yourself to keep going. The accumulation has crossed an internal threshold. This realization doesn't lead to panic.

It leads to grief.

Not loud grief. Quiet grief: grief for the version of you who entered this work expecting effort to lead somewhere coherent, grief for the belief that endurance would eventually be rewarded with resolution. You don't voice this grief easily. It feels indulgent. Others have it worse. You know that. You've told yourself that for years, and that comparison has been useful.

It has also been silencing.

You start to see how repetition without repair narrows the future. Not dramatically, but in small ways. You imagine fewer possibilities. You make plans with more contingencies. You lower expectations not just for outcomes, but for meaning. You don't dream about the work anymore.

You manage it.

Someone asks about your long-term plans. Where do you see yourself in a few years? You hesitate. Not because you don't have options, but because you don't know which version of yourself those options assume—the one shaped by accumulation, or the one that existed before it.

This is the limit. Not collapse.

Recognition.

The point where you can no longer pretend repetition is neutral, or adaptation cost-free. You see clearly now that something has been building, and it's asking to be addressed. This part of the journey doesn't tell you what to do next.

It tells you what you can't ignore.

The work has been forming you. The question is whether you'll continue to let it do so without intention. By the end of this chapter you haven't reached a breaking point.

You've reached awareness.

You understand that repetition, left unexamined, can quietly hollow out meaning even as competence remains intact. You also understand something else: awareness creates choice. Not easy choices.

But real ones.

Chapter 8—**Leadership and Moral Exposure**

When Authority Increases, Protection Does Not

The decision lands on your desk late in the day—not because it's urgent, but because no one wants to be the one to send it earlier. It's been circulating quietly, discussed in side conversations and half-formed emails, each iteration softened and deferred. Now it's yours.

You read it carefully. Then again. On paper, it makes sense. The rationale is clean. The constraints are real. The language is careful in the way organizations get careful when they know an outcome will hurt someone but can't admit that directly. You understand why the decision is being made.

That doesn't make it easier to hold.

You think immediately about who will be affected. Not in the abstract. Not as a category. Specific people come to mind. You picture their faces. You know where they'll be standing when they hear the news. You can already imagine the questions, the pauses, the look someone gets when they're waiting for a better answer than the one you're about to give.

You close the document. You don't have to decide whether you agree with it. That part already happened somewhere else. Your role now is to carry it.

The meeting is scheduled for the next morning. You arrive early, as usual. You arrange the chairs, review the agenda, take a few steadying breaths—not because you're nervous, but because you know this will require containment. People filter in. There's small talk. Familiar jokes. The ordinary rhythms of a team that trusts you.

You feel the weight of that trust.

When the moment comes, you explain the decision. You use clear language. You acknowledge impact without dramatizing it. You name constraints honestly. You answer questions directly. You watch the room carefully, because the room will tell you when the truth has landed. You see understanding turn into disappointment. You see posture change, shoulders drop, people lean back as hope leaves the conversation.

Someone asks if there's any flexibility. You shake your head. Someone asks if this could change later. You explain why it won't. The questions slow. No one raises a voice. No one storms out. By every measure, the meeting goes well.

That's what others will say later.

Afterward, people thank you for being straightforward. "I know that wasn't easy," someone says. You nod and accept it. You appreciate the acknowledgment. You also notice how quickly the room empties. People have tasks to return to. Work that still needs doing. The decision is finished for them. For you, it isn't—you can feel that immediately, the way you can feel a bruise before it shows.

Later that day, one person comes to see you privately. They close the door behind them. They don't argue or ask you to change anything. They just want to talk through what this will mean for them.

You listen, answer carefully, resist the urge to reassure in ways you can't guarantee. You stay present.

When they leave, they thank you again. "You handled that well," they say. You sit alone for a moment after the door closes and feel the familiar tightening—part fatigue, part responsibility, part something else you still don't have words for.

That evening, you replay the meeting, not to second-guess the decision, but to make sure you didn't miss anything you should have said differently. You didn't. You did exactly what the role required.

That's what unsettles you.

Leadership changes the timeline of moral impact. Earlier in the work, decisions could end when the interaction ended. You could step away and say, truthfully, that the outcome wasn't yours to carry. Now decisions follow you. They show up in emails weeks later, in quiet hallway comments, in the way someone avoids your eyes or lingers when they need to ask something else. You're reminded repeatedly.

You don't get to close them.

You also notice that people assume you're okay with it—not because they're careless, but because you look capable. You've learned how to project steadiness even when you're holding something that doesn't sit right. You don't correct the assumption. You don't know how.

A few days later, someone outside your team asks how things are going. You give the summary version: busy, complicated, moving forward. They nod. They understand. You don't mention the decision, or the weight, because there doesn't seem to be a place for that in casual conversation.

You think about how leadership has changed your relationship to the work. You still care deeply. You still believe in what you're doing. You are also more exposed than you've ever been to the moral fault lines of the system. You see where decisions land, who absorbs the impact, and how often there's no way to make things whole. You're responsible for navigating that reality without letting it fracture the team.

That night, the clarity arrives quietly: authority hasn't insulated you from moral injury. It has positioned you closer to it—closer to the moments where values and constraints collide, closer to long-term consequences of decisions that made sense in isolation, closer to outcomes you can't fully stand behind but must stand with.

You don't regret stepping into leadership. You would make the choice again. But you understand now that leadership doesn't mean carrying less. It means carrying differently, and unless that weight has somewhere to go, it will settle in you whether you acknowledge it or not.

Leadership Doesn't Buffer the Work

Leadership is supposed to make things easier. That's the assumption, anyway: more experience, more authority, more influence. From the outside, it looks like a buffer, a layer of protection earned through years of doing the work well.

From the inside, it rarely feels that way.

You don't step into leadership all at once. It happens gradually. You're asked to take on a little more responsibility here, a little more decision-making there. Someone notices your steadiness, your judgment, your ability to hold complexity without unraveling.

You say yes. It feels like a natural progression.

At first the shift is subtle. You're still in the field, still present with people, still doing the work you've always done. But now you're pulled into side conversations, asked for input before decisions are finalized, expected to anticipate problems rather than only respond to them. You're closer to the levers.

You're also closer to the consequences.

The first time you feel the difference, it catches you off guard. A decision needs to be made quickly. There isn't a good option, only a least-worst one. You weigh factors, consider impact, choose. The team moves on.

Later you realize you're the one replaying it.

Others have already shifted attention to the next problem. For them, the decision is done. For you, it's still alive, like something you set down but can't stop hearing.

You start to notice how leadership concentrates moral exposure. As a frontline responder, you carried the weight of individual interactions. As a leader, you carry patterns. You're responsible not just for what happens in front of you, but for what will happen because of what you decide. The scale changes.

The insulation does not.

You are now the one explaining decisions you didn't design: policies handed down from elsewhere, constraints imposed by funding, logistics, politics, timelines that look reasonable on paper and collapse on the ground. You're expected to make these decisions legible to your team and humane to the people affected by them.

You're good at that.

That's why you were asked.

The cost shows up quietly. A responder comes to you after a difficult interaction. They're upset. They want to understand why the system keeps failing the same people in the same ways. You listen, validate, explain. You don't tell them how many times you've had this conversation. You don't tell them you share their frustration.

You absorb it.

You also notice how often people assume you're holding up fine. You're calm. Decisive. You don't escalate unnecessarily. You project confidence even when you're uncertain. From the outside it looks like resilience.

From the inside it looks like containment.

There's a meeting where you're asked to defend a decision you don't fully agree with—not because it's indefensible, but because it's incomplete. You explain rationale, acknowledge limitations, emphasize constraints. You do not say what you wish were possible instead. There isn't space for that.

Afterward someone thanks you. "You made it sound reasonable," they say. You nod. You know what they mean. You also know what it cost: the quiet translation of an ethically thin decision into language people can live with.

Leadership changes how and where moral injury occurs. It doesn't remove it.

It relocates it.

You are less exposed to individual stories and more exposed to cumulative impact. You see downstream effects across weeks and months. You watch moral residue build from choices that made sense in isolation and did harm in aggregate.

You don't have a mechanism for resolving that.

Authority hasn't given you the ability to fix what's broken. It has given you a front-row seat to how broken things are—and responsibility for carrying that knowledge without alarming others.

At the end of a long day you review notes, emails, messages, and realize how much of your energy has gone into translating between worlds: policy and practice, leadership and frontline staff, systems and people. You're good at translation, but it's exhausting in a way that doesn't register as fatigue.

You think back to earlier in your career, when leadership meant influence. You're beginning to understand it also means exposure—exposure to moral complexity, decisions with no clean resolution, knowing too much and being able to change too little.

This is the point where some leaders harden. They stop engaging the moral dimensions and focus on metrics. They distance from impact. They protect themselves by narrowing their field of concern. You've seen it. You understand the temptation.

You also know what it costs.

For now, you're still here, trying to lead with integrity—trying to hold the work's moral center even as your role pulls you toward efficiency and away from direct contact. You haven't resolved the tension.

You've stepped into it more fully.

Leadership hasn't made the work easier. It has made the moral stakes more visible, and you're only beginning to understand what that visibility will ask of you.

Carrying What Others Can't

Leadership changes who gets to set things down.

As a frontline responder, you were allowed moments of release. You could step outside after a hard interaction. You could trade shifts. You could say, honestly, "That one stayed with me." As a leader, those permissions quietly disappear—not because anyone forbids them, but because the role doesn't make room for them.

You begin to notice how often people bring their hardest moments to you. A responder knocks after a difficult interaction. They're shaken, angry, confused. They need to talk it through before they can continue. You listen, slow them down, help them make sense of what happened. They leave steadier than when they arrived.

You remain.

Another time, a volunteer pushes past protocol trying to help someone in crisis. The intention was good. The impact is complicated. You're asked to address it. You speak carefully: you honor the desire to help, explain the boundary crossed, absorb the discomfort so it doesn't spread. Later you replay the conversation and wonder whether you asked too much of them. You wonder whether the system asked too much of you.

You notice how often leadership requires translating pain into something manageable. You take raw frustration and turn it into process. You take anger and redirect it into policy. You take grief and make it fit into a timeline. This isn't manipulation. It's containment.

It keeps the work moving.

It also accumulates.

Over time you realize leadership positions you as a moral buffer. People bring you what they can't carry. You hold it so they can keep functioning. You don't resent this. It's part of the role you accepted.

What you didn't anticipate was how little opportunity there would be to pass it on.

You can't unload downward. You're careful not to burden the people you supervise. You don't want to destabilize them or undermine their confidence. You don't unload upward easily either. Those above you are managing their own layers, and there's an unspoken expectation that you'll bring solutions, not additional strain.

So you carry it.

The effect isn't dramatic. It's steady pressure, an internal crowding. You're always holding something just out of sight, something unresolved that doesn't have a clear place to land. You're still effective, still respected, and increasingly alone with the moral weight of the work.

A responder says, "I don't know how you do this." They mean it as a compliment. You smile. You don't know how to answer, because you aren't sure you are doing it in a way that's sustainable.

You also realize how often leaders are expected to model resilience without revealing cost. You're supposed to project steadiness, confidence, perspective. You can acknowledge difficulty in abstract terms, but not in a way that suggests it might be changing you. You learn to speak about stress without naming strain, and you become fluent in that language.

At some point you notice you've stopped checking in with yourself the way you encourage others to do. You ask your team how they're holding up, what they need. You rarely ask yourself the same questions—not because you don't care, but because you don't know where the answers would go.

Leadership doesn't just increase responsibility.

It redistributes vulnerability.

You absorb uncertainty so others can feel grounded. You carry unresolved moral tension so the work can continue. That absorption is rarely acknowledged, rarely named, rarely repaired. You think back to earlier responses when you could say, "That decision wasn't mine." Now, even when it isn't technically yours, it feels like it is. You're the one explaining it, justifying it, living with its impact.

This is one way moral injury shifts in leadership. It becomes less about a single violation and more about prolonged exposure; less about one moment and more about sustained responsibility for imperfect systems. You can't opt out.

You can only decide how consciously you carry it.

By the end of this part, you haven't found a solution. You've found recognition: leadership isn't only influence and authority. It's what you hold so others don't have to, and the cost of that holding deserves to be seen.

When Leaders Stop Carrying It Alone

For a long time, you assume this is simply how leadership works. You absorb. You translate. You contain. You don't question it because questioning it feels like weakness, or worse, irresponsibility. People are counting on you. The work is fragile. You don't want to be the one who drops something others can't afford to pick up.

So you keep carrying it.

The shift doesn't happen because you plan it. It happens because something makes continuing this way impossible—not dramatic enough to justify stepping away, not urgent enough to demand intervention, just persistent enough that you can no longer pretend it's sustainable. You notice you're slower to recover after hard days. Decisions follow you home more often. You're holding conversations in your head long after they've ended. You're still functioning.

You're not fine.

The first crack comes through another leader, not someone above you but someone beside you. You're in a meeting that has already gone long. The agenda is full. The decisions are complicated. Everyone is tired. Someone names a concern you've been carrying quietly for months. You expect the room to move past it.

Instead, another leader says, "I'm struggling with that too."

The room stills—not because it's dramatic, but because it's rare. You feel relief first. Then fear. If this is spoken aloud, what happens next?

No one rushes to fix it. No one reframes it into something safer. The conversation doesn't spiral. It deepens. Others nod. Someone adds detail. Someone names a cost they haven't said out loud before.

The work doesn't collapse.

The team doesn't lose confidence.

Something shifts anyway.

Later you realize what demonstrated itself in that moment: the moral weight didn't disappear.

It redistributed.

You begin, carefully, to test this. Not by unloading everything. Not by turning meetings into confessionals. Just by naming reality when it's already present. "This decision sits uncomfortably for me," you say once, in a room that can handle it. You don't justify it. You don't dramatize it. You let it stand.

The room adjusts.

You discover people are more capable than you assumed—not of fixing the problem, but of holding it with you. You had been protecting them from that burden. You're no longer sure that protection was necessary.

This doesn't mean everything becomes easier. There are still moments you must absorb and contain. Leadership still requires discretion. Some decisions can't be shared widely. But now there are places where the moral reality of the work can land, and that makes a difference.

When you stop carrying everything alone, your leadership changes. You listen differently. You speak more plainly. You stop over-polishing decisions that are ethically thin and instead name their limits directly. This doesn't undermine authority.

It strengthens credibility.

People trust leaders who are honest about constraint more than leaders who pretend coherence exists where it doesn't.

You also notice your internal world feels less crowded. The decisions don't echo as long. The conversations don't replay as heavily—not because they matter less, but because they've been witnessed.

You begin to understand that moral injury in leadership is often sustained by isolation. Not physical isolation.

Moral isolation.

The belief that you must hold the full weight of imperfect systems without sharing the strain, because doing so would destabilize others. That belief turns out to be only partially true.

When leaders stop carrying it alone, something subtle changes in culture. People speak more honestly about constraints. Decisions are framed with more humility. Moral tension becomes something that can be acknowledged rather than denied. It doesn't solve the system.

It humanizes it.

You become more attentive to other leaders too. You check in differently. You ask questions that go beyond performance. You listen for what isn't being said: the containment, the quiet fatigue, the practiced composure that hides accumulation. You don't rush to fix it.

You offer presence.

By the end of this chapter, leadership hasn't become safer. It has become more honest. You still hold authority. You still carry responsibility. You still make decisions that sit imperfectly with your values. What's changed is this: you no longer believe you're meant to hold all of that alone.

Leadership doesn't protect you from moral injury.

It exposes you to it differently.

What determines whether that exposure becomes injurious or survivable isn't strength, skill, or silence. It's whether the moral reality of the work has somewhere to go.

Chapter 9—**Team Dynamics and Shared Strain**

The Uneven Load

Teams are supposed to distribute the weight. That's the promise, anyway. You're not alone out there. You have roles, coverage, handoffs—people who know the pace, the language, the pressure. You can lean on each other, and you do.

But over time, you notice something nobody says out loud: the strain doesn't distribute evenly.

It shows up in small ways first—who stays late without being asked, who volunteers for the difficult conversation, who gets pulled aside when someone is upset because "he's good with people." Who becomes the person others route conflict toward because he can absorb it without escalating. The pattern is familiar once you see it. Some people do the visible tasks. Some people do the invisible ones.

In the field, invisible work has a particular shape. It's the responder who stands at the edge of the room scanning not for supply gaps but for emotional temperature. The one who notices a volunteer about to snap and steps in with a question that slows the moment down. The one who catches a survivor before they walk out—not because the process changed, but because leaving alone would cost them more. None of this is in the job description. It's still required.

At first, teams appreciate it. They rely on it. They comment on it: "You're really good at keeping people calm." "You're the one who can talk people down." "I'm glad you're here." It feels like affirmation. It is. It also becomes assignment.

Certain roles gravitate toward certain people—not always by choice, but by reputation. The steady ones get sent into the hardest interactions. The calm ones get placed where tension will peak. The ones with pastoral presence get asked to handle grief, anger, despair—not as an official role, but as a function of who they are. Over time, the team stops asking whether that person has capacity. They assume.

There's a moment on a response when someone on your team looks shaken after an interaction. Nothing dramatic—no shouting, no threats. Just a quiet conversation that ends with a survivor breaking down in a way that catches the responder off guard. They step away, trying to regain composure. A supervisor notices and says, "Go find him."

It isn't a request. It's a reflex.

You're the one who can hold that.

You find the responder outside near the back of the building, where the air feels cooler and the noise doesn't land as sharply. You don't start with advice. You start with presence. "What happened?" They tell you, haltingly at first and then faster, like the words have been trapped. They describe the survivor's face, the way the story landed, the moment they didn't know what to say. "I feel stupid," they say. "I didn't know what to do."

You tell him he isn't stupid. You tell him the moment was hard. You remind him that not knowing what to say is part of the work. As you speak, you feel his body settle—breathing steadier, shoulders dropping back into place. He thanks you and goes back inside.

You return to the floor. No one asks how you're doing. They assume you're fine. They assume the role you played for him is neutral for you.

That's the uneven load: the person who helps others regulate becomes the one who rarely gets to. The person who carries other people's intensity becomes the one whose own intensity has to stay contained. The team needs stability, and stability ends up housed in particular bodies.

You begin to see how shared strain can still be lonely. You're surrounded by people. You're functioning inside a team with support structures. And yet certain experiences keep finding the same person—not because anyone intends harm, but because teams under pressure default to what works. A hard situation arises. Someone glances toward you. They don't even say your name. You feel the pull, step in, handle it, and keep the work moving.

Later someone says, "We couldn't do this without you." They mean it as gratitude, and part of you receives it that way. Another part hears what's underneath: We couldn't do this without you carrying what we can't.

Officially, teams talk about capacity. There are shift limits, break schedules, rotation plans. People are encouraged to rest, to step away when they need to. In practice, the invisible work bypasses those safeguards because it isn't measured, because it doesn't look like labor, because it happens in the cracks.

You feel the consequences in yourself not as collapse but as narrowing. You start anticipating where you'll be needed before anyone asks. You brace for the emotional spikes. You conserve words and warmth, keeping something in reserve because you know the moment is coming when the team will look to you. It doesn't make you less effective. It makes you more careful.

And it shapes relationships. When people only see you as steady, they stop checking whether steadiness has a cost. You become the person others offload onto without realizing they're offloading. You become the place where intensity goes to be managed.

At some point you notice a newer responder mirroring the pattern. They see how the group functions, who carries what, and they begin stepping into the same kinds of moments—trying to be useful, trying to belong. You watch it happen and feel something tighten, because you know where it leads.

Nothing has exploded. No scandal, no confrontation, no dramatic rupture. Just a truth becoming clear: teams can share tasks and still concentrate moral strain. And if that concentration goes unnamed, it doesn't disappear. It settles deeper into the people who carry it.

What Can Be Said

Every team has rules—not the written ones in manuals or orientation decks, but the ones you learn by watching what happens when someone speaks and what happens when they don't. You learn them fast, because the work doesn't leave much room for mistakes.

The first rule is usually about tone. You can talk about frustration as long as it stays light. You can name exhaustion as long as you smile. You can admit something was hard as long as you follow it with reassurance: "I'm wiped, but it's all good." "That was rough, but we'll manage." "I need a minute, then I'm back in." These are acceptable—even encouraged. They signal awareness without disruption.

You also notice what happens when someone steps outside the boundary. A responder tries to name something heavier, not dramatically, just honestly: "I don't think that interaction was okay," or "I'm having a hard time with how that decision landed." The room gets quieter—not hostile, careful. Someone offers a practical response: "Did you take a break?" Someone reframes it: "These situations are always tough." Someone moves the conversation forward: "Let's circle back to assignments."

The moment passes. The message lands: that kind of truth doesn't belong here.

You don't take it personally. You understand why it happens. Teams in crisis environments run on momentum, and emotional containment keeps the work functional. No one wants to open something they can't close before the next wave hits. So the rules make sense.

They also have consequences.

Over time you become fluent. You can feel when a conversation is open and when it's already closed. You learn which supervisors are safe for certain truths and which ones will redirect. You start editing yourself mid-sentence, choosing not to say something because you can already hear how it will be received. You call it discernment. It is. It's also self-protection.

There's a moment in a debrief when someone asks, "Anything else we should know?" It's a genuine invitation. You feel the familiar internal inventory begin: what would help, what would matter, what would it cost to say? You offer something neutral—true, but incomplete—and the meeting moves on. Later you realize you never even considered saying the thing that mattered most. You didn't censor it. You bypassed it.

This is how silence becomes skilled. It isn't fear-based; it's adaptive. You learn to protect yourself and the group at the same time by keeping certain experiences internal. You don't feel dishonest. You feel efficient. Teams often mistake this for cohesion: everyone appears aligned, conflict stays low, decisions get implemented smoothly. From the outside, the team looks strong. From the inside, something else is happening. Certain experiences never get shared. Certain reactions never get mirrored. Certain questions never get asked—not because they're inappropriate, but because there's no container for them.

Support also tends to flow in predictable directions. When someone is visibly upset, the team rallies. When someone looks overwhelmed, people step in. When someone is quiet but functioning, they're left alone. Silence reads as capacity. Functioning reads as resilience. The quieter you become, the less support you receive.

Humor plays its part too—often skillfully, rarely cruelly. Gallows humor releases pressure without opening anything deeper. It creates quick bonds in back rooms and cars and late-night corners. You participate. Everyone does. And sometimes you notice how humor arrives right before something important could be said: the comment lands close to truth, someone cracks a joke, and the moment closes.

There's a particular loneliness in being surrounded by people who care while still not being able to say what is actually sitting in you. You're not isolated. You're filtered. Only certain parts of you are allowed into the room.

You see the cost most clearly when someone leaves. Quietly. They stop taking shifts, transfer roles, step away without much explanation. Afterward people say, "They never really said anything," or "I didn't know they were struggling," or "They seemed fine." You know why: they followed the rules, so no one saw it coming.

You begin to understand that teams don't always lack care. They lack language. They don't know how to talk about moral strain without destabilizing themselves, so they default to what they can manage: stress, fatigue, workload. Those are real. They're also safer.

At some point you catch yourself enforcing the rules without meaning to. A teammate starts to say something heavier than usual, and you feel the impulse to redirect—to reassure, normalize, close it down. "It's been a long week." "We're all feeling it." "Let's just get through today." The moment closes. You don't feel proud or guilty.

You feel practiced.

The hardest part is that these rules aren't enforced by authority. They're enforced by care. No one wants to burden others. No one wants to be the reason the team slows down. No one wants to open something they can't help carry. So everyone carries their piece quietly. The team stays functional. The cost accumulates individually.

There are cracks, though: a late-night conversation, a car ride back from site, a quiet corner after shift. Someone asks, "Can I say something that might sound bad?" You nod. They speak. The truth lands between you, unpolished and real, and you don't fix it. You don't reframe it. You let it exist. Those moments are rare. They matter. They don't usually make it back into the room.

By now you can see it clearly: teams can be deeply supportive and still structurally silent. They can care and still lack the capacity to hold certain kinds of truth. That doesn't make them unsafe. It makes them incomplete. And it makes leadership matter—not authority, but presence. Leaders who can tolerate discomfort without rushing to resolution, who can say, "Yeah, that doesn't sit right," without explaining it away, create space. Not many are trained to do this.

Without space, the rules persist:

Say what can be solved.
Name what can be managed.
Carry the rest quietly.

You didn't write these rules. You learned them. Now you live inside them.

The question isn't whether these rules exist.

It's what they cost over time—and who ends up paying.

When the Weight Shows

It doesn't announce itself. There's no single moment where the team realizes something has been off for a while—no dramatic failure that forces recognition. What happens instead is quieter and more confusing.

One of the steady ones falters.

It might look like irritation that comes out sharper than expected, a missed detail that normally wouldn't happen, a delayed response that would once have been automatic. Nothing catastrophic—just enough to register. Someone asks, "Are you okay?" They mean it. The steady one nods and says yes, and the team accepts the answer because the work needs to keep moving.

What's difficult is that the visible slip is rarely the problem. It's the signal. By the time it shows, the weight has already been there for a long time.

The team responds the way teams know how to respond. They adjust coverage, offer time off, suggest a break. "You've been carrying a lot," they say. "You need to take care of yourself." All of that is appropriate. All of it is partial, because what's being addressed is capacity, not meaning.

You notice how quickly the situation becomes individualized. The language shifts: they're tired, they're overwhelmed, they need rest. No one asks what they've been carrying for everyone else. No one asks how long the team relied on them without noticing.

Often the person who faltered feels embarrassed—not ashamed exactly, exposed. They're used to being the steady one, the one others lean on, the one who absorbs strain without making it visible. Now the strain is visible, and they apologize. "I'm sorry," they say. "I don't know what came over me."

You want to tell them they have nothing to apologize for. You don't always know how.

The team reassures them. "You're human." "It happens to everyone." "We've got you." The words are meant to help. They also gently redirect attention away from what made the moment necessary in the first place.

Sometimes the falter isn't sharpness. It's withdrawal. The steady one stops volunteering for hard conversations and becomes harder to find when tension rises. They do their assigned tasks and little more. From the outside it looks like disengagement. From the inside it feels like preservation. People notice and don't know what to do with it: "They've changed." "They used to be so on top of things." "I hope they're okay."

The unspoken question hangs there: what happened to them?

What's hard to say is that nothing happened—nothing new. What happened was accumulation: the quiet work of holding, the repeated absorption of moral weight, the steady translation of harm into language the system could tolerate. Eventually the container fills.

When the weight shows, teams often scramble, not because they don't care but because they don't have a framework for what they're seeing. They treat it as an anomaly rather than a predictable outcome. They look for quick fixes: "Take some time off." "Switch roles for a while." "Step back from the front line." These can help. They often don't reach the deeper issue, because the issue isn't simply exposure.

It's violation.

There's a particular isolation when a team responds to moral strain as if it were simple fatigue. The person experiencing it feels not unseen, but misunderstood—offered solutions to a problem they aren't having. The team returns to equilibrium, the work continues, and the uneven load redistributes—often onto someone else.

Sometimes the steady one leaves. Quietly. Another role, reduced availability, no more deployments. The team is surprised. "We didn't know they were thinking about leaving." "They never said anything." You know why.

They followed the rules.

After they're gone, the work still gets done. It always does. Someone steps into the space they left, and the system absorbs the loss. But something shifts anyway. The team feels thinner.

What rarely happens is collective reflection. There's no pause to ask: what did they carry for us, how did we rely on them, what made it impossible to put that weight down? Those questions don't fit into operational debriefs. They don't have metrics. They don't resolve quickly.

So when teams lack language for moral strain, it shows up sideways—in turnover, disengagement, cynicism, quiet resentment. The steady ones don't always burn out. Sometimes they just leave, or harden, or go silent. And you begin to see the difference between shared workload and shared witnessing. When witnessing doesn't happen, the work still gets done.

The cost just goes somewhere else.

There is no neat repair at the end of this chapter. What ends here is illusion: the illusion that strain distributes itself fairly, that steadiness is free, that teams can rely on silence without consequence.

In the next chapter, we'll turn toward what becomes possible when teams begin to treat moral strain not as an individual weakness, but as shared responsibility—and what it takes to build containers strong enough to hold it.

Chapter 10—**What Leaders Hold Back**

The Weight of What You Don't Say

Leadership doesn't just change what you carry. It changes what you're allowed to reveal.

At some point—without anyone naming it—you realize part of your role is to protect others from information that would destabilize them. Not false information. Not lies. The truth, carefully portioned. You notice it the first time you decide not to say something: the information is accurate and relevant, and it would explain why the situation feels the way it does. It would also land with more force than the team can absorb right now.

You look at the room. People are tired, focused, doing their best to keep moving. They need clarity, not complexity; direction, not doubt. So you simplify. You offer what's necessary, not what's complete. The work continues. You tell yourself you made the right call.

You probably did.

Leadership teaches you that transparency isn't absolute. It's contextual. You begin making decisions about who can carry which truths, and when. You learn that timing matters as much as content—that some truths, delivered too early or too openly, don't empower. They destabilize.

So you hold them. You don't think of it as concealment. You think of it as stewardship.

There's a meeting where funding is discussed more bluntly than usual. You hear how narrow the margins are, how contingent the next phase will be, how little room there is for error. Someone says, "We'll need to manage messaging carefully." You understand what that means. Later, when the team asks what's coming next, you speak with measured confidence. You talk about plans and contingencies and flexibility. You don't mention how close the system is to failing them. They nod, orient, and keep working.

You've done your job.

You also feel something settle in your chest.

Before leadership, you were protected from certain kinds of knowledge. After leadership, you become the buffer. You are the place where uncertainty stops. That doesn't make uncertainty disappear. It relocates it.

You start getting questions you can't fully answer: "Is this going to keep going like this?" "Are we going to have enough staff?" "Is this decision really going to hold?" You hear the fear beneath the words, and you choose reassurance that is technically accurate but incomplete. You emphasize what can be done rather than what might not be. You watch tension ease, just enough.

That easing has a cost.

Leadership requires morale management, not through speeches but through regulation—tone, pacing, and what you allow into the room. You begin to live in the narrow gap between honesty and containment. And you realize you can't vent easily in either direction: upward, because you're expected to translate concern into solutions; downward, because your job is to steady, not unburden.

So you hold. You find places to set things down quietly if you can—a trusted colleague, a late-night walk, a notebook no one reads. If you don't find those places, the weight doesn't vanish.

It accumulates.

You also learn that silence at this level is rarely about fear. It's about protection. You don't want to alarm people unnecessarily, fracture trust, or introduce doubt that will ripple outward and land on people already stretched thin. So you edit. You curate. You contain. The danger is subtle: containment can become concealment without you noticing the shift—not because you intend to mislead, but because the work moves more easily when complexity stays hidden. You tell yourself you'll say more later.

Later keeps moving.

A staff member you trust asks you directly, "How bad is it, really?" You see the crossroads clearly. You could answer fully and invite them into the uncertainty you're carrying, or you could protect them from it. You choose protection: enough to orient, not enough to overwhelm. They thank you, and you wonder what it would have been like to answer differently.

Leadership isolates not because you're above others, but because you hold information that has nowhere to go. You can't discharge it downward without risk. You can't always discharge it upward without consequence. So it stays with you. You're praised for "keeping things together," which often means keeping complexity from spilling out. You do it well. The system rewards you for it.

No one asks what it costs.

And there's a specific fatigue that comes from speaking with certainty you don't feel—not dishonesty, performance. You choose settled words so others can act. You keep doubts internal. You postpone your own processing so the work can continue. It doesn't make you less sincere.

It makes you more alone.

By the end of this part, nothing has gone wrong. The response is functioning. The team is steady. The work is moving. From the outside, everything looks fine. From the inside, you're beginning to understand that holding back is its own form of exposure—and you don't yet know how long you can do it without something giving.

When Containment Breaks

Containment works until it doesn't. Not because you stop caring or lose discipline, but because there are limits to how much unspoken truth one person can hold without consequence. Those limits aren't announced. They're discovered—usually too late to pretend you didn't know they were there.

The first crack isn't dramatic. You answer a question too quickly. Your voice carries an edge you didn't intend. Someone looks at you a second longer than usual, registering that something is off. You correct yourself, smooth it over, and keep going.

But you notice.

There's a particular exhaustion that comes from constantly translating reality into something survivable for others. You aren't just managing logistics. You're managing impact—filtering what people are allowed to feel, when they're allowed to feel it, and how much they're allowed to know. This isn't manipulation.

It's protection.

And protection takes energy.

You see the crack most clearly when someone asks a question you've been holding an answer to for too long—not because you don't know how to answer, but because you know too well: "Is this actually going to get better?" "Are we really set up to keep responding like this?" "What happens if the next phase doesn't materialize?" You hear how much trust is in the question. You feel the weight of deciding what they can safely carry. You hesitate.

That hesitation is new.

Sometimes containment breaks outward. You say more than you meant to—not recklessly, just enough that the room changes temperature. You name fragility instead of smoothing it away. People sit up straighter. Someone exhales sharply. Someone looks at the floor. You wonder if you said too much.

Afterward, someone pulls you aside. "I'm glad you said that," they tell you, or, "That was hard to hear, but I appreciate the honesty." You nod, and you watch how quickly the system moves to stabilize: follow-up messages soften edges, clarity is restored, containment resumes.

Only now it resumes with memory.

Other times containment breaks inward. You stop translating altogether. You get more concise, more guarded. You keep explanations strictly functional, avoid unnecessary conversations, narrow your emotional range. From the outside it looks like professionalism. From the inside it feels like hardening. Hardening is efficient. It reduces friction and prevents further leakage of moral complexity into spaces that can't hold it. It also costs you access to parts of yourself you used to rely on. Curiosity narrows. Empathy becomes more selective. You disengage not because you don't care, but because caring has become expensive.

You notice how tempting it is to stay there.

Many leaders do. They don't announce it. They just get quieter.

There's a moment when you recognize the path in real time. Someone expresses concern about a decision—careful, respectful, saying what you once would have said. You feel irritation rise, not at them but at the risk, at the reopening. You almost shut it down.

You catch yourself.

That pause matters.

The other option is breaking silence intentionally. Not everywhere, not all at once, but in chosen spaces with chosen people, in language that doesn't overwhelm but doesn't disappear either. It requires discernment without self-erasure: knowing when truth builds capacity rather than fractures it, and tolerating discomfort rather than eliminating it.

So you experiment. You name impact alongside outcome. You acknowledge the moral weight of a decision alongside its necessity. You say, "I don't love this, but this is where we are." You don't dramatize it or apologize. You refuse to make the cost invisible.

The room grows quieter than usual.

Something shifts.

Not everyone responds well. Some people want certainty, not honesty. Some interpret your openness as weakness. You feel the pull to retreat back into containment. But others breathe easier. They speak more honestly. They stop blaming themselves for reactions they didn't have language for.

You realize containment didn't just protect them from fear.

It also protected them from truth.

Breaking silence doesn't mean saying everything. It means saying enough that you're no longer carrying it alone. It means refusing the lie that steadiness requires invisibility. It means trusting that adults can hold more truth than systems often allow.

You also learn limits. Some rooms still can't hold it. Some people aren't ready. Some truths land harder than intended. You don't become naïve.

You become intentional.

By the end of this part, you haven't solved the problem. You've named it. You've seen containment has limits, and disclosure has risks. What matters is you're no longer pretending neutrality. Leadership will cost something either way.

The question isn't how to avoid the cost, but how to distribute it more honestly.

After the Silence Breaks

Nothing resolves cleanly after truth is named. There is no moment where you finally say the thing you've been holding and the system exhales, realigns, and moves forward healed. What happens instead is slower and messier and more uncertain.

Which is exactly why it matters.

After you stop containing everything, the work feels different. Not lighter—more exposed. You become aware of your own language: when you're choosing it, when you're smoothing something that deserves to stay rough. You don't lose skill. You lose the illusion that skill can make moral tension disappear. You begin speaking with a different kind of care—not less professional, less evasive.

The team notices too, gradually. Some become more cautious, listening closely as if recalibrating what kind of leader you are now. Others seem relieved. They begin asking questions that aren't just operational: "Do you think that was the best we could do?" "Does this bother you too?" "Is there a reason this keeps happening?" They ask tentatively. You hear the risk in it.

Trust shifts when leaders stop performing certainty. For some, it's destabilizing. They relied on you to absorb doubt so they didn't have to feel it. When you stop, they carry more. They may resist. They may long for the smoother version of leadership.

You feel that pull too. It would be easier to go back.

For others, trust deepens. Not because you have better answers, but because you're not pretending to have answers you don't believe in. They stop wondering what you're hiding. They stop blaming themselves for reactions they couldn't explain. Something loosens.

The work doesn't slow down as much as you feared. It changes texture. Meetings take longer. Conversations linger. Decisions feel heavier because their cost is acknowledged instead of buried. And responsibility begins to spread.

When leaders name moral strain, teams start seeing it as part of the work rather than a flaw in an individual responder. That shift changes how people interpret frustration, grief, and withdrawal. It interrupts the reflex to internalize harm as failure. You see it in small ways: someone says, "That didn't sit right with me," and no one rushes to fix it. Someone asks to rotate not because they're tired, but because they've been carrying too much of one kind of interaction. Someone names a limit without apology.

These aren't revolutions. They're openings.

The process is uneven. Some engage; others retreat. Naming truth doesn't guarantee change.

It creates possibility.

Leadership becomes less about direction and more about containing discomfort—the ability to let things remain unresolved without rushing to closure, to sit with moral ambiguity without collapsing into defensiveness or despair. You intervene differently: less smoothing, more holding. When someone names moral tension, you don't immediately redirect to solutions. You say, "Yes. That's real."

Sometimes that's enough.

You also remain discerning. There are still rooms where certain truths overwhelm rather than empower. Urgency still wins at times. You aren't pretending otherwise. Over time, you see what this kind of leadership does. It doesn't remove strain; it changes where it lives. Instead of settling silently in individuals, it becomes something the group can see, even if they don't yet know what to do with it.

This is where moral injury either deepens or begins to shift. Private strain isolates. Strain named without support overwhelms. Strain shared carefully creates the possibility of repair—not resolution, repair.

You realize leadership was never about having the answers. It was about deciding what to do with what you know: who carries it, who doesn't, and whether the cost stays hidden or becomes shared. There is grief here—grief for the ease of certainty, for the version of leadership that looked steadier from the outside, for the belief that being dependable meant being untouched.

You let that grief exist.

And you feel something else too: a quieter integrity. Not because the work has perfectly aligned with your values, but because you've stopped pretending it has. By the end of this chapter, the work is still demanding. Constraints still exist. Decisions still hurt. What has changed is the direction of silence.

It no longer only flows inward.

It no longer concentrates exclusively in you.

That doesn't make leadership easier.

It makes it more honest.

What comes next is not comfort. It's capacity: the capacity to stay without disappearing, to lead without hardening, to let others see the cost so they don't have to imagine they're carrying it alone. This is not the end of moral exposure.

It's the beginning of moral sharing.

When You Are the One They Blame

It happens sooner than you expect—not right after you start speaking more openly, not in the first meeting where you name the cost. It comes later, when the consequences of that openness have had time to travel.

You return to a site that feels tense in a way you now recognize. Not chaotic—tight. People are doing their jobs, but conversations end faster. Eye contact lingers longer. You feel it before anyone says anything.

The confrontation doesn't happen publicly. It happens at the edge of the day when most people have left and the space has that hollowed-out feeling after urgency recedes. Someone asks if they can talk to you "for a minute." You say yes.

You always do.

They don't sit. "That decision you talked about earlier," they say, arms crossed. "You made it sound like there wasn't another option." You nod. "There wasn't," you say carefully. "Not a viable one." They shake their head. "I don't buy that."

No yelling. No drama. Just direct disagreement. Your body responds anyway.

They keep going. "You told us you wanted honesty. You said we should name the impact. So I'm naming it. That decision hurt people. And now we're the ones dealing with the fallout." You listen. You let them finish. They aren't wrong. They aren't entirely right either. That's what makes it hard.

You explain the constraints again—funding limits, staffing realities, tradeoffs locked in before the decision reached your level. You don't hide behind policy. You don't pretend you weren't involved.

You own what you can.

They listen, jaw tight. "So why does it feel like we're the ones paying for it?" they ask.

You don't have a clean answer.

This is the part no one prepares you for: when you stop hiding the strain, you also stop absorbing blame invisibly. People can see where decisions live now. They can see you. You chose visibility.

This is part of what that costs.

They tell you about families, the anger they absorbed, the sense of being set up to fail. You recognize the story from your own years, just from another angle. You don't interrupt. You don't defend. You let them say it. "I don't think you did this to us on purpose," they say finally. "But I don't think you protected us either."

The sentence hits because a part of you knows it's true. You protected the system. You protected momentum. You protected morale. You didn't protect them from impact. You couldn't.

"I couldn't protect you from this," you say slowly. "I wish I could have."

They look for an apology, a solution, a reversal. You offer none of those. You offer acknowledgment. You offer the truth that you are also carrying this. It doesn't satisfy them.

It shouldn't.

After they leave, you sit alone longer than you meant to. Not criticized—seen. Your decisions aren't abstract anymore. They have a face and a voice and a cost you can't redistribute. Later someone higher up checks in. "I heard there was some pushback," they say. You keep it neutral. You name concern, not conflict. They nod. "That's tough," they say. "Just make sure the team stays focused."

Focused. The word lands with familiar weight.

That night the conversation replays—not because you regret what you said, but because you recognize the cost of saying it. People will come to you now. They'll bring anger, disappointment, even betrayal. Some will be fair. Some will not.

All of it will land.

You consider, briefly, whether silence would have been easier. It would have been. It also would have kept you intact at the expense of everyone else. Leadership isn't choosing the option without cost. It's choosing which cost you're willing to carry.

The next day you show up anyway. You listen more carefully, explain more slowly, and don't rush past moments of tension even when they make you uncomfortable. You also notice something else: a few people look at you differently. Not with blame—with trust. They know you won't disappear behind policy. They know you won't pretend things are fine when they aren't. They know you'll take the weight when it comes.

That trust is heavier than praise.

You're also more vulnerable. Opacity no longer protects you. You can be challenged, questioned, held accountable in ways that are personal, not procedural. It's not safer.

It's more honest.

Over time you learn that being blamed isn't the same as being wrong. Sometimes it's the price of being visible. Sometimes it's the cost of refusing to let harm remain abstract. You learn to distinguish between criticism that requires adjustment and anger that needs witness. You don't always get it right.

You keep trying.

By the end of this chapter, leadership no longer feels like a shield or a pedestal. It feels like a place where moral weather hits first—where truth, once spoken, has consequences that don't resolve neatly, and where choosing integrity doesn't guarantee approval.

What you understand now is simple, and not easy: when leaders stop hiding the cost of the work, the cost doesn't vanish. It becomes shared—sometimes unevenly, sometimes painfully, always imperfectly.

But no longer invisibly.

And that, however difficult, is the only way this work stays human without asking the people who do it to disappear.

Chapter 11—**Staying Without Disappearing**

The Question You Avoid

You don't ask it right away. You've seen what happens when people ask too soon—when the work is still loud and urgent and there's no space for anything but action. The question would feel indulgent then, out of sync with what's needed. So you wait. You keep responding, keep showing up, keep doing what you've always done—only now with a sharper awareness of what it costs. You tell yourself that awareness is enough, that naming the strain privately will keep it from accumulating.

For a while, it almost works. Then, on a day that isn't dramatic at all, the question surfaces anyway:

How do I stay without disappearing?

It doesn't arrive as panic. It arrives as practicality. You're reviewing your calendar—responses, meetings stacked on top of each other, stretches of time that will be consumed by other people's emergencies—and you notice that you don't feel dread exactly. You feel calculation: How much do I have to give right now? What can I absorb this week? What will this cost me later? You've always made calculations, but they used to be logistical. Now they're personal. You don't judge the shift. You just notice it.

Staying has never been the hard part. You're good at endurance. You know how to push through fatigue, manage stress, function inside chaos. You've built an identity around reliability. People count on you. You count on yourself. Disappearing is quieter. It doesn't look like quitting; it looks like narrowing. Fewer parts of you show up. Less curiosity. Less softness. More efficiency. You've seen it happen to others, and you can feel it beginning in you. That's what makes the question unavoidable.

You think back to when you first started—not the details of the disasters, but what it felt like to enter them. There was fear and uncertainty, yes, but also openness: a sense that the work would shape you in ways that mattered. You didn't expect it to be easy. You also didn't expect it to require so much quiet self-editing. Over time, you learned which reactions were "useful" and which were not. You learned to manage your face, your tone, your body language. You learned to stay composed even when you felt shaken. These were skills, and they served you well.

The trouble is that skills, overused, turn into constraints.

You notice it most clearly in moments of connection. Someone starts to tell you something real—not a crisis, just something personal. You listen. You respond appropriately. And you feel a thin distance between what you're offering and what you're feeling. You're present, but you're holding back. Not out of disinterest—out of habit. You've learned that staying open costs more than it used to.

The work has trained you to compartmentalize. You can move from devastation to normal conversation in minutes. You can hear impossible stories and still remember to ask about logistics. You can be fully present in one space and leave it cleanly enough to function in the next. This ability is praised. It's called professionalism. What no one tells you is that compartmentalization doesn't disappear when you don't need it. It becomes a default. You start applying it to your own life without realizing it—setting aside not just other people's pain, but parts of yourself that feel inconvenient or costly.

This is how disappearing begins.

You don't want to romanticize any of this. Some containment is necessary. You can't feel everything fully and still do the work. You can't carry every story home intact. The question isn't whether to contain. It's whether containment has begun to replace presence altogether. You see the tension in how you rest. When you take time off, you don't always feel restored. Sometimes you feel unmoored. Without the structure of urgency, things surface that you didn't have time to notice—restlessness, flatness, the uneasy question of whether you've forgotten how to be without being needed. That thought makes you uncomfortable.

You speak about this carefully, if you speak about it at all. You don't want to sound ungrateful. You still believe the work matters. What you're questioning isn't the mission. It's the version of you the mission seems to require. You hear echoes of the question in others, too—not stated directly, but in sentences like: I don't feel like myself anymore. I love the work, but something feels off. These aren't burnout statements. They're identity statements. They're about erosion, not exhaustion.

At some point, you realize the question isn't whether you should leave. It's whether staying has to mean disappearing—whether commitment requires self-erasure, whether the only way to endure is to become smaller. You don't believe that's true. You just don't yet know what the alternative looks like.

So you start paying attention to people who have stayed a long time and still seem whole. Not untouched. Not light.

Whole.

They have boundaries, but not walls. They speak honestly without being reckless. They don't rush past moral discomfort, but they don't drown in it either. They've built lives that don't orbit entirely around the work. They protect parts of themselves that have nothing to do with response. They don't apologize for that. You realize it isn't accidental.

Staying without disappearing isn't about better self-care. It's about integration—refusing to split yourself into "work self" and "real self" so completely that one of them starves. It's letting the work change you without letting it consume you. That's harder than it sounds.

The work will always ask a lot: flexibility, availability, emotional labor, moral courage. It will ask you to show up when others can't. What it doesn't have the right to ask for is your invisibility. You begin to understand that staying well isn't a private achievement. It's relational. It depends on whether there are places where you can be fully human without performing competence—people who know what you're carrying and don't rush you to put it down or push through it, spaces where you can name strain without it being framed as failure.

You don't solve this all at once. You begin with small refusals. You stop minimizing when someone asks how you are. You stop pretending endurance is effortless. You choose presence over polish in a few key relationships. The relief that brings is quiet, but real. By the end of this part, the question hasn't gone away. What's changed is that you're no longer treating it as evidence that something is wrong with you. You're starting to believe it's a legitimate question—a sign that you care enough about the work, and about yourself, to want a way forward that doesn't require erasure.

That belief is fragile. It's also essential.

What Actually Helps

Once you stop avoiding the question, you want answers—not slogans, not wellness advice that sounds good but doesn't survive contact with the work. You're not looking for inspiration. You're looking for something that holds. What actually helps is quieter than you expected.

The first thing that helps is telling the truth about what doesn't. You've tried what people recommend. You exercise. You take days off when you can. You step away between responses. Some of it helps your body. Very little touches the deeper strain. You stop pretending that means you're doing it wrong. You realize no amount of rest will resolve a problem that isn't primarily fatigue. That recognition alone eases something.

What helps next is distinguishing boundaries from limits. You're good at boundaries—saying no to extra shifts, protecting time, stepping back before overload. Those skills keep you functional. Limits are different. Limits are about what you will no longer carry silently. You begin to notice when you're absorbing moral strain that doesn't belong entirely to you—when you're translating harm so thoroughly that no one else has to feel it, smoothing decisions so completely that you're the only one left holding residue. You start asking a new question:

Does this need to be carried alone?

Sometimes the answer is yes. More often than you thought, it isn't.

One of the first limits you set is conversational. You stop answering "How are you?" automatically—not everywhere, not with everyone, but with a few people you trust. You answer honestly enough to register. It was hard. That one stayed with me. I'm okay, but I'm carrying more than usual. You don't dramatize. You don't unload. You simply refuse to disappear behind competence. You're surprised by how often the other person doesn't recoil. They lean in.

Another thing that helps is letting go of the idea that you should be able to process this alone. You've been trained to be self-contained—to regulate, to not need too much from others, especially when everyone is stretched. Taken too far, that training becomes isolation. So you look for spaces where moral complexity is welcome—not problem-solving spaces, but witnessing spaces. Places where you can say, That didn't sit right, and no one rushes to fix it, reframe it, or move past it. These spaces are rare. When you find them, you protect them.

You also learn that who you speak to matters as much as what you say. Some people rush to reassurance. Some rush to advice. Some normalize in ways that flatten the experience. What helps are people who can tolerate unfinished sentences—who don't need the work to make sense in order to stay with you in it. You stop expecting this from everyone. You stop offering your inner life to people who can't hold it. This isn't withdrawal. It's discernment.

Another thing that helps is reclaiming parts of yourself the work doesn't touch—not as escape, but as balance. You invest in relationships and activities that don't ask you to be competent, steady, or useful—places where you can be clumsy, quiet, unsure. It feels unfamiliar at first. You've gotten used to being needed. Being unnecessary takes practice. Over time, something returns in small doses: spontaneity, curiosity, play. Not constantly.

Enough.

You also begin to change how you show up at work—not your commitment, but your posture. You stop rushing to make everything okay. You stop absorbing discomfort before it has a chance to be shared. When appropriate, you name moral strain out loud: That was hard. I don't love that decision. This is sitting with me. You don't demand solutions. You just refuse invisibility. Sometimes the room stays quiet. Sometimes someone else speaks. Either way, you feel less alone.

You learn that staying without disappearing requires rhythm—not constant intensity, not constant withdrawal, but movement. You rotate roles when you can. You take breaks before you're depleted. You pay attention to what kind of strain you've been carrying and for how long. You stop treating yourself like an unlimited resource. You start treating yourself like part of the system—something that requires care and maintenance.

Eventually, what helps most is letting go of the fantasy that staying well is an individual achievement. You can't out-resilience a morally demanding system. You can only stay human within it if there are others willing to do the same. You begin thinking less about coping and more about culture: Where is it safe to tell the truth? Who names cost without being punished? What gets rewarded? What gets silenced? Staying without disappearing isn't only about what you do; it's about what's possible where you are.

That doesn't mean you wait for the system to change before you take care of yourself. It means you stop pretending the system is irrelevant. You advocate where you can. You model what you wish were normalized. You support others when they risk honesty. You don't fix the culture.

You influence it at the edges.

There are still days when the question resurfaces. Now it feels less like a threat and more like a compass—pointing to where you're giving too much in ways that hollow you out, where it's time to ask for help, step back, or speak up. It doesn't demand one answer. It invites ongoing attention.

By the end of this part, you don't have a formula. You have anchors: truth-telling, discernment, shared witnessing, reclaimed selfhood, rhythm. They don't eliminate cost. They make it survivable without erasure.

When Leaving Is the Right Thing

You don't want this part to be true. You'd rather believe that if you pace yourself, tell the truth, build support, show up with integrity, you'll be able to stay—that there's always a way to adjust without walking away.

Sometimes there is. Sometimes there isn't.

You notice it first as a narrowing of options. You've tried what helped before. You've named strain. You've shifted roles. You've taken breaks. You've asked for what you need. You've done the honest work of staying without disappearing—and still, something essential feels at risk. Not your energy.

Your values.

There's a moment—often quiet, almost ordinary—when you realize continuing would require a kind of numbness you're not willing to cultivate. You're in a meeting, or on a site, or in a conversation you've had many times. A decision is being discussed. You can see the impact clearly now. You know who will absorb it. You know how the explanation will land. You also know what it would take to keep doing this.

You would have to stop caring in a way you can't reverse.

The knowledge arrives with surprising calm.

Leaving is rarely about one incident. It's about accumulation: the number of times you've been asked to enforce what you don't believe in; the number of times you've named cost and watched it go nowhere; the number of times you've been told—explicitly or not—that integrity is negotiable if efficiency requires it. Eventually, the ledger doesn't balance.

People outside the work often misunderstand this. They assume leaving means you couldn't handle it, that you burned out, that you failed to manage stress or set boundaries. Those explanations are tidy. They're also incomplete. Sometimes leaving is the most honest response available.

You notice how different it feels from exhaustion. You're not depleted.

You're clear.

You're not running from the work. You're stepping away from a version of it that asks too much of the wrong things. You grieve, because of course you do—relationships, identity, purpose, competence, the world's need. That grief doesn't make the decision wrong. It makes it real.

You may try to talk yourself out of it. You remind yourself of the good—people helped, moments that mattered. You wonder if you're being too rigid, too idealistic. You take the questions seriously. That's part of your integrity. Eventually, another question becomes louder:

What will it cost me to stay?

You imagine yourself five years from now if nothing changes. Honestly. Not as threat, but as forecast. You picture the version of yourself who has learned to live with misalignment by shrinking—hardening, going quiet, letting certain parts go numb. You recognize that person. You don't want to become them.

In this context, leaving isn't rejection. It's refusal: refusal to disappear in order to remain; refusal to trade moral clarity for continued access; refusal to let the work take more than it can give back. That refusal isn't disloyal. It's accountable—to yourself.

You may not announce the decision at first. You create distance. You say no more often. You explore adjacent roles. You imagine other ways to contribute that don't require the same compromises. You notice your body's response: sadness, yes, and also relief.

When you tell people, reactions vary. Some understand immediately. They're carrying similar questions. Others are surprised. You were one of the steady ones, the ones who could handle it. You let them believe what they need to believe. You don't owe anyone a justification.

There may be pressure to stay "just a little longer"—finish this response, see the project through, wait for conditions to improve. You consider these requests carefully. Sometimes they're reasonable. Sometimes they're a way for the system to postpone reckoning. You learn to tell the difference.

Leaving doesn't erase what you've given. It doesn't undo the good. It doesn't mean the work no longer matters. It means you've decided that how you live matters too. You carry the work with you—just not at the center of your life. What surprises you is how much stays: skills, awareness, capacity to witness without turning away. They show up differently—in quieter ways, in places that don't require you to disappear in order to belong.

You begin to see leaving not as the opposite of staying, but as part of the same continuum. Both require honesty. Both require courage. Both ask you to listen carefully to what the work is asking—and to decide, deliberately, what you can and cannot give.

By the end of this part, there's no prescription. Some people will stay, and staying will be right. Some people will leave, and leaving will be right. What matters isn't the choice. It's whether the choice is made with integrity rather than erosion—whether you remain visible to yourself in the process, whether you trust your worth isn't measured by how much you endure.

The work will go on. It always does. The question is not whether it survives without you. The question is whether you survive the work without losing what makes you human. Sometimes the most faithful response is to stay and insist on a different way.

Sometimes it is to leave and carry what you've learned into places where it can breathe.

Both are forms of care. Both require moral courage. And neither should require you to disappear.

The Moment You Know

It isn't dramatic. That's what surprises you. You always assumed that if leaving were the right thing, there would be a clear rupture—collapse, confrontation, something decisive enough to justify it. Instead, the moment arrives quietly, without spectacle. You almost miss it.

You're back from a response that looks, on paper, like many others. Nothing catastrophic. Nothing that would raise concern. You did your job. You were competent. You were steady. People thanked you. You accepted it. Now you're home, unpacking your bag—boots by the door, jacket hung where it always goes. Routine. Muscle memory. Halfway through, you stop. Not because you're tired.

Because you don't want to put the bag away.

The realization is immediate and physical, a subtle resistance—as if completing the routine would mean consenting to something you haven't agreed to yet. You stand there longer than necessary. You recognize the feeling: the pause before responses lately, the quiet internal bracing, the sense that something is being asked before it's been acknowledged. This time, you don't override it.

You sit down instead. The house is quiet. There's nothing urgent demanding your attention. For once, there's space. And in that space, the thought arrives fully formed:

I can't go back like this.

Not I can't go back. Not I'm done. Just like this. The distinction matters.

You try to reason with it. This wasn't the worst response. You've handled harder. Everyone has days when it feels heavier. Maybe it passes if you rest, recalibrate, adjust. These are good arguments. They don't move the feeling, because the feeling isn't about capacity.

It's about consent.

You replay the response, not looking for mistakes but for moments where something shifted. A meeting where a decision was treated as settled even though you knew it wasn't right. You didn't speak up—not because you didn't see it, but because you already knew the outcome. A conversation where you chose efficiency over honesty because honesty would open something you didn't have the authority to hold. A moment of being thanked that brought tightening instead of relief.

None of this is new. What's new is how clearly you can see the lack of room to be yourself inside it—not the professional version of you, but the human one.

You realize staying would require a deeper numbing than you're willing to do. Not all at once. Gradually. The kind that feels like adaptation until you notice how quiet everything has become inside you. You know this path. You've watched others walk it. You don't judge them. You just know you don't want to follow.

The clarity is almost peaceful. There's grief—of course there is—for the work, for the people, for the version of you who believed it could be sustainable without this cost. But there's also relief. Not because you're escaping.

Because you're finally listening.

You don't tell anyone right away. This isn't a decision yet. It's recognition. You let it sit for days, weeks, testing itself against your life. You notice what your body does when you imagine staying unchanged: tightness. You notice what happens when you imagine stepping back: space. That difference matters.

You keep working for a while. You show up. You do your job. Nothing outward changes. Inside, something has already shifted. You stop forcing yourself through moments that feel wrong. You name limits internally instead of rationalizing them away. You pay attention to how often you feel relief when something is canceled or delayed. You don't shame the relief. You respect it.

Eventually, something confirms what you already know. You're asked to take on a responsibility that would have once felt like an honor. You hear yourself hesitate. You imagine saying yes, imagine the cost, imagine the version of yourself you'd have to become to do it well. You realize you don't want to become that person.

You say no.

It feels clean.

That's when you understand the decision has already been made—not impulsively, not reactively, but quietly over time, through attention. Leaving, if it comes, will simply make visible what has already shifted. You grieve. You let the grief be honest—meaning, purpose, relationships, identity, the certainty of being needed. You don't rush it. You don't minimize it.

What surprises you is how intact you feel underneath it. You are not broken. You are not depleted. You are not leaving because you failed. You are leaving because you succeeded in noticing when the cost crossed a line.

Later, people will have opinions. Some will call it self-care. Some will call it burnout. Some will admire your courage. Some will wonder, quietly, if they should ask themselves the same questions. You let them. You don't correct the narrative.

You know what this is.

The moment you know isn't loud. It doesn't demand announcement. It simply refuses to be ignored. And once you honor it, you realize that staying without disappearing was never primarily about endurance. It was about listening—listening to what the work asks, listening to what it takes, listening to what you can no longer give without losing something essential.

By the time you actually leave, if you do, the leaving may feel almost anticlimactic. The real change already happened. You stayed present long enough to hear yourself. You trusted that voice. You chose not to disappear.

That choice stays with you, no matter where you go next.

Chapter 12—**Repair Is Not a Program**

What Healing Actually Looks Like

Repair doesn't begin where most organizations look for it. It doesn't start with a framework, a toolkit, or a new line in a strategic plan. It doesn't arrive through a workshop or a policy revision, no matter how well-intentioned. Those things can help, sometimes. But they are not where repair begins.

Repair starts in places that don't scale—moments that don't look impressive from the outside—when someone notices harm and refuses to rush past it.

You learn this slowly, usually after you've tried everything else. You've attended the trainings. You've implemented the recommendations. You've sat through sessions on resilience and wellness that offered useful language but never quite reached the thing you were carrying. You've filled out surveys about stress, capacity, and workload. Some of it helped.

None of it repaired what was strained, because what was strained wasn't just energy. It was trust: trust in the work, trust in the system, and trust that your values still had a place here. You can't restore that with a checklist.

You see it most clearly when someone tries to treat moral injury as if it were burnout. The solutions look familiar—more time off, better rotation, clearer boundaries, improved communication—and all of these matter. All of them can make a real difference. And still something remains unresolved, because moral injury isn't primarily about overwork.

It's about being required, again and again, to act against what you believe is right—or to witness that violation without recourse.

You can rest and still feel that dissonance. You can be well-supported and still feel misaligned.

The first time you hear someone speak honestly about this, it isn't polished. It's hesitant. They don't use clinical language. They don't frame it as a problem to be solved. They say something like, "I don't know how to explain this, but something about that didn't sit right with me."

The room goes quiet—not uncomfortable, attentive—and you feel recognition in your body before your mind catches up. That's it, you think. That's what's been missing.

Repair begins when that sentence is allowed to stand. Not reframed. Not redirected. Not fixed. Just held. Someone nods. Someone else says, "Yeah. I felt that too." Another person exhales, relieved they're not the only one.

Nothing has been solved. Something has been acknowledged. The air in the room changes.

And you realize how rare that is.

So often, conversations rush toward solutions because sitting with harm feels inefficient. Organizations convert discomfort into action items. Moral truth that doesn't point cleanly toward improvement gets edged out. Repair requires slowness, and that alone makes it countercultural in disaster work.

You remember a debrief that went differently than most—not because the response was easier or the outcome better, but because someone asked a different question: "What did this ask of us that we weren't prepared for?" The room stilled. People stopped talking about logistics and timelines and started talking about moments: conversations that stayed with them, decisions they understood but didn't agree with, the weight of being thanked when nothing had been fixed.

No one corrected anyone else. No one tried to make it okay.

You left that room feeling tired and steadier at the same time.

That was repair.

Repair doesn't erase harm; it changes your relationship to it. When moral strain is named and witnessed, it stops isolating. It becomes shared, even if it remains unresolved. That sharing doesn't make the work lighter, exactly.

It makes it more honest.

And honesty is one of the few things that stabilizes people over time.

It also becomes easier to recognize what isn't repair. Repair is not a mandatory check-in that people learn to perform. It's not a box to tick before moving on. It's not asking, "Is everyone okay?" and treating silence as confirmation, because silence is often compliance, not comfort.

Repair asks different questions: What stayed with you? What felt wrong, even if it was necessary? What are we carrying forward from this? These questions don't have clean answers.

That's the point.

Repair almost always happens in small groups: a hallway conversation after the meeting ends, a late-night call with someone who doesn't rush you, a moment of honesty between colleagues who trust each other enough to drop the script. These moments are fragile. They depend on psychological safety—easily disrupted by hierarchy, urgency, or fear of consequence. They can't be mandated.

They have to be protected.

Over time, the pattern becomes clear: repair is relational before it is structural. Policies can reduce harm. They can't repair it. Only people can do that—people willing to witness without fixing, to stay present without rushing, to tolerate the discomfort of unresolved moral tension.

That kind of presence is rare.

It's also teachable.

You start noticing the leaders who made it possible. They didn't have all the answers; they simply didn't disappear when things got complicated. They named difficulty without defensiveness. They admitted limits. They didn't pretend necessity erased harm.

They didn't make it better. They made it bearable.

You also remember the times repair didn't happen: when concerns were acknowledged and then buried; when people were told, "That's just part of the job"; when moral strain was reframed as personal weakness or lack of resilience. Those moments didn't end the work.

They ended trust.

Repair is slow. It doesn't fit neatly into after-action reports. It doesn't show up in metrics. It doesn't always lead to visible change. But it accumulates. Each time harm is named and not dismissed, something strengthens. Each time someone feels less alone in what they're carrying, the work becomes slightly more sustainable.

By the end of this part, you understand something important: repair is not a program you implement. It's a practice you choose, again and again. It requires time you don't think you have. It requires courage you may not feel ready for. It requires letting go of the fantasy that everything can be fixed if you just move fast enough.

Repair asks you to slow down long enough to tell the truth.

Making Space Where There Isn't Any

The hardest thing about repair is not knowing how to do it. It's finding a place for it in environments built to move, not to pause.

Disaster work runs on urgency. Decisions are made quickly because delay has consequences. People are trained to act, prioritize, triage. Slowing down can feel irresponsible—even dangerous—so when someone suggests making space for reflection or moral processing, the instinctive response is resistance.

There isn't time. There are too many needs. We'll come back to this later.

Later rarely comes.

You see the tension most clearly in the spaces between tasks. Debriefs are tight. Meetings are packed. Check-ins are designed to surface issues that can be addressed immediately. There's an unspoken rule: if it can't be fixed, it shouldn't take up time.

Moral strain doesn't fit that rule.

It isn't fixable in the moment. It doesn't resolve cleanly. It often raises more questions than answers. So it gets edged out.

Making space for repair doesn't mean building long, formal processes. It means changing how you use the space you already have. Small openings appear: the last five minutes of a meeting, the pause before the next agenda item, the walk back to the car after a site closes. These moments are usually filled with logistics or light conversation.

They don't have to be.

You experiment carefully. Instead of asking, "Any questions before we move on?" you ask, "Did anything today sit wrong with you?" You don't push. You don't explain. You let the question land.

Sometimes no one answers, and that's okay. The question itself does something. It signals that moral experience belongs here, even if it isn't spoken yet.

Other times, someone speaks quietly: "It was hard telling that family no." "I'm still thinking about that decision." "I don't know why, but that interaction bothered me."

Your job in that moment is not to manage the emotion.

It's to let it be named.

Making space turns out to be as much about restraint as initiative. The instinct to reassure is strong: "You did the best you could." "That's just how it is." "At least we helped someone." These responses comfort in the short term. They also close the space too quickly. So you practice holding silence a few seconds longer than feels natural. You resist the urge to tidy up the conversation.

It takes discipline.

It builds trust.

Hierarchy complicates this. People speak differently when supervisors are present. They calculate risk. They choose words carefully—or not at all. Repair happens more easily when power is acknowledged rather than ignored. When a leader says, "I don't have answers for this, but I want to hear it," the room changes. When they admit a decision caused harm even if it was necessary, people feel less alone.

Safety is not the absence of authority.

It's the presence of humility.

Repair also can't be rushed. If someone names a moral wound, the next step isn't action planning. It's listening. You don't need to agree. You don't need to resolve. You don't need to promise change you can't deliver.

You need to stay.

That staying does more than any policy revision could.

Over time, urgency becomes negotiable—not eliminated, renegotiated. You start distinguishing between what truly can't wait and what feels urgent because no one has made room for it before. You realize ignoring moral strain doesn't save time.

It borrows time from later, with interest.

There are risks. Naming harm can surface anger, grief, or frustration you don't have the resources to address fully. Some conversations will feel messy. Some will remain unresolved. Some will leave people unsettled.

That doesn't mean they were harmful.

It means they were honest.

You also learn to protect these spaces. You don't allow them to be co-opted into performance. You don't turn them into required ritual. You don't measure them for productivity. Once repair becomes something people are evaluated on, it stops being repair.

It becomes compliance.

Making space often means choosing what not to do. You shorten an agenda. You cancel a nonessential update. You let a meeting end without resolution. These choices feel risky at first. Over time, you see the payoff: people show up differently when they believe their moral experience will be taken seriously—less defensive, less withdrawn, and more willing to stay engaged even when the work is hard.

Repair doesn't require consensus. It requires acknowledgment. Two people can experience the same decision differently and both be telling the truth. Repair doesn't force alignment.

It allows plurality.

And that alone reduces harm.

By the end of this part, you understand making space for repair isn't about adding something new. It's interrupting the reflex to move on. It's resisting the idea that urgency excuses silence. It's choosing—again and again—to make room for the human cost of the work, even when that cost doesn't point neatly toward improvement.

What Leadership Can—and Cannot—Do

By the time repair becomes visible, leadership is already involved. Not always formally or by title, but by influence and tone—by what's permitted and what isn't. Repair either survives or collapses based on what happens next. That puts leaders in an uncomfortable position: not because they're responsible for everything, but because they are responsible for what becomes possible.

One of the hardest truths for leaders to accept is this: you cannot repair moral injury for someone else. You can't talk them out of it. You can't fix it with better messaging. You can't resolve it by explaining why a decision was necessary. Trying to do so often makes it worse, because moral injury isn't confusion.

It's clarity without recourse.

What leaders can do is protect the conditions under which repair becomes possible, and that begins with restraint. The urge to respond quickly is strong—to reassure, justify, or show competence by having an answer. Most leadership training rewards that impulse. Repair asks for something else: leaders who can tolerate being seen without solutions.

That isn't weakness.

It's credibility.

You've seen leaders who do this well. They listen without interrupting. They acknowledge harm without qualifying it. They say, "I hear what this cost," or, "I don't have a way to make this right, but I don't want to pretend it didn't matter." Those statements don't fix anything, but they change everything because they tell people they don't have to carry the moral weight alone.

You've also seen the opposite: leaders who respond to moral strain with explanations that may be accurate but land as dismissal; who emphasize necessity so thoroughly that harm disappears from the story; who treat discomfort as misunderstanding rather than conflict. These leaders are often well-intentioned.

They're also unsafe—not because they cause harm on purpose, but because they leave no room to name it.

One of the most important practices is resisting personalization. When someone names moral distress, it's rarely an accusation. It's a signal. Leaders who hear it as critique become defensive; leaders who hear it as information become curious.

Curiosity keeps the conversation open. Defensiveness shuts it down.

Another critical practice is naming limits honestly. Not everything can be changed. Not every harm can be repaired. Pretending otherwise erodes trust faster than admitting constraint. When leaders say, "I can't fix this," without disappearing or deflecting, something stabilizes.

People don't expect perfection. They expect honesty.

Leaders shape repair by what they model. If you rush past moral discomfort, others will too. If you treat it as inconvenience, others learn to hide it. If you acknowledge it and stay present, others follow. Culture doesn't shift because of memos.

It shifts because of imitation.

There is also a boundary leaders must hold. Repair does not mean unlimited processing in every space. It does not mean turning operational meetings into therapy sessions. It does not mean requiring vulnerability. Leaders protect repair by containing it rather than dispersing it everywhere: choosing appropriate spaces, setting expectations, and ensuring those who speak are not punished for doing so.

That isn't softness.

It's stewardship.

Leaders also need repair, and that's part of what complicates this. When leaders isolate and absorb moral strain without support, they harden. They become less available, less curious, more brittle.

Repair requires leadership to be relational too. Leaders need places where they can name cost without collapsing authority—rare spaces that must be protected intentionally.

Over time, leadership here starts to look like a function, not a title. Anyone who shapes what is sayable is exercising leadership. Anyone who reinforces silence or challenges it is influencing culture. Anyone who stays present to moral strain without rushing it away is leading.

By the end of this part, it's clear: leadership can't guarantee repair, but it can make it possible. In morally demanding work, that may be one of the most important things leaders ever do.

What Changes When Repair Is Real

Repair doesn't announce itself with relief, and it doesn't feel like closure. Most of the time, you only recognize it in hindsight—when you realize something that once broke people no longer does, or at least doesn't do so as completely.

You see it when the same kind of moment happens again: a difficult decision, a constrained outcome, a conversation where the answer is still no. The circumstances haven't improved. What's changed is how the cost is carried. This time, when the decision lands, there's space afterward—not performative space, not a scheduled debrief with the wrong questions.

Just room.

Someone says, "That didn't sit right with me," and no one rushes to correct them. Someone else adds, "Yeah. I felt that too." The moment doesn't spiral. It doesn't derail the work. It doesn't require resolution.

But it doesn't disappear either.

Later, you notice what this does to people. They don't withdraw as much. They don't harden as quickly. They don't carry the same quiet resentment home. The harm still exists; what's different is that it's no longer invisible.

Repair works this way: not by removing moral strain, but by redistributing it. What was carried privately becomes shared. What was internalized becomes speakable. What was mistaken for personal weakness is recognized as structural demand. That redistribution doesn't lighten the work, exactly.

It keeps people intact inside it.

You see it in retention, not dramatically but in small ways. People stay a little longer. They don't vanish without explanation. When they leave, they leave with clarity rather than collapse. They talk about why, and they aren't rewritten as "burned out" or "not cut out for it."

They're honored as people who paid attention.

You also see it in how new responders are shaped. When moral strain is named early, it stops being a shock later. Newer staff don't assume they're doing something wrong when discomfort shows up. They don't pathologize their response to misalignment. They learn unease can be information, not failure, and that knowledge alone prevents harm.

Repair changes how mistakes are held. When something goes wrong, the conversation doesn't jump straight to blame or justification. There's room to ask not only what failed, but what this asked of people. That question doesn't excuse error.

It contextualizes it.

Over time, teams who practice repair speak differently. Less polished. More precise. They don't hide behind language or pretend decisions are painless. They don't require cheerfulness as proof of commitment. They trust each other more because they've seen each other stay when things were hard to name.

Repair doesn't prevent moral injury.

It interrupts its isolation.

Instead of accumulating quietly, strain is surfaced earlier. Instead of being absorbed alone, it is carried in relationship. Instead of eroding identity, it becomes part of a shared narrative about what this work costs. That difference is everything.

You realize repair isn't the opposite of urgency; it's what makes urgency survivable. Without repair, urgency burns through people. With repair, urgency still demands—

—but it doesn't consume.

And you understand why repair can't be a program. Programs end. Repair doesn't. It has to be renewed each time harm is acknowledged instead of dismissed, each time someone stays present instead of moving on too fast, and each time truth is allowed to land without being neutralized. That choice is made daily, often quietly, often without recognition, which is why repair is rarely credited. It doesn't produce deliverables.

It produces people who can keep going without disappearing.

By the end of this chapter, you understand something essential: moral injury is not inevitable, and neither is repair. Both are shaped by culture, leadership, and everyday choices. Repair doesn't fix the system. It makes life inside the system more honest, more humane, and more sustainable.

In the next chapter, we'll step back and tell the truth about the cost of this work—not to discourage those who do it, but to honor them. Because silence was never neutrality, and naming the cost was never weakness.

It was always the beginning of care.

Chapter 13—**Telling the Truth About the Cost**

No one teaches you how to talk about the cost.

They teach you how to prepare—how to deploy, how to triage, how to stay professional when things are chaotic, painful, or unfair. They teach you how to hold yourself together in front of people whose lives have just come apart. What they don't teach you is how to speak honestly about what the work takes from you, especially when the work still matters and you still believe in it.

So you learn indirectly. You notice which stories are welcomed and which fade out mid-sentence. You hear how some experiences are framed as "hard but meaningful," while others are quietly redirected toward gratitude or growth. Over time you absorb an unspoken rule: difficulty is acceptable, but only if it resolves quickly or can be translated into something useful.

The complication isn't policy. It's tone.

You don't want to sound ungrateful. You've seen what happens when no one shows up, when systems fail completely, when care is absent. You also don't want to sound fragile. You've worked hard to be competent, reliable, steady. People depend on you. You depend on yourself. And you don't want to burden others. Everyone is already carrying too much. Adding your experience to the pile can feel selfish, indulgent, beside the point.

So you choose your words carefully. You talk about long days. You talk about staffing and resources. You talk about being tired. You describe the work in ways that are accurate but incomplete, leaving out the parts that don't fit easily into conversation.

At first, this feels like professionalism.

Later, it starts to feel like you're disappearing in plain sight.

You remember the first time you tried to say something closer to the truth. Not dramatic, not emotional—just precise. "That one stayed with me." Or, "I don't know why, but that didn't sit right." You weren't accusing anyone. You weren't asking for anything. You were naming an experience.

The response wasn't hostile. It was brief: a nod, a quick explanation, a reminder of constraints. Then the conversation moved on. No one told you not to say it.

They just didn't invite you to keep going.

That's how silence becomes culture. Not through policy, but through repetition. Moral discomfort gets reframed as stress. Necessary harm gets explained until it sounds weightless. People get praised for composure, for pushing through, for keeping things moving. None of this requires bad intent. It requires momentum, and momentum has a way of turning omission into habit.

From the outside, the field looks strong: capable, resilient, able to absorb extraordinary strain. From the inside, many people are carrying experiences they don't know how to talk about, let alone share, and they assume it must be personal.

Everyone else seems to handle this. Maybe I'm overthinking it. Maybe I care too much.

These thoughts are common. They are also unnecessary.

The truth is not that you are failing. The truth is that this work costs something—not because it's done poorly, but because it is morally demanding. You are asked to act with care inside systems that cannot fully honor that care. You are asked to be present to loss you cannot repair. You are asked to translate limitation into something humane, again and again, often without acknowledgment.

That costs something.

Pretending it doesn't doesn't make you stronger.

It makes you alone.

Telling the truth about the cost doesn't mean turning every conversation into a confession. It doesn't mean complaining. It doesn't mean abandoning professionalism or commitment. It means refusing the idea that silence equals strength. It means recognizing that naming cost isn't disloyalty.

It's an ethical act.

You understand this the first time someone else finally says what you've been carrying. Not loudly. Not as a demand. Just accurately: "That decision made sense," they say, "but it hurt."

No one rushes to correct them. No one accuses them of being unrealistic. The room goes quiet for a moment, and in that quiet people breathe. Nothing has been solved, but something has been acknowledged, and that acknowledgment changes the air.

When cost is named, it stops leaking out sideways as cynicism, withdrawal, or numbness. It stops getting mistaken for personal weakness. It becomes visible—shared, real. The work doesn't fall apart.

If anything, it steadies.

Still, you see why truth-telling feels risky. Once you name cost, you can't unname it. You can't go back to pretending the work is hard only because of hours or logistics or funding. You can't unknow how often moral compromise is built into the system. Naming changes perception, and perception changes responsibility. Even when nothing changes structurally, something changes relationally: people have to decide whether they will acknowledge what's already happening.

And telling the truth can be misread. You worry it will sound like complaint, like criticism, like a lack of gratitude for the good the work still does. You worry it will be interpreted as blaming people who are also constrained, also trying their best. You don't want to disrupt morale. You don't want to slow things down. You don't want to make already hard work feel heavier.

So you soften, or you stay silent.

You've also seen what dismissal looks like. Someone speaks honestly, and the response is a well-meaning explanation. Or a reminder of necessity. Or a reframing that relocates the problem back into personal coping.

"You did what you could."

"That's just part of the job."

"Try not to take it personally."

None of these are cruel. They're efficient. They close the space before the truth has anywhere to land.

There's also the risk of exposure. Once you say the cost out loud, you step out from behind competence. In a field that prizes steadiness, that can feel dangerous. You wonder whether you'll still be trusted, still be relied on, still be seen as capable. Those fears aren't imagined.

They're learned.

And there's a subtler risk: if you name cost, people may bring their cost to you. They may expect you to hold space, to listen, to carry more. You already feel stretched. You wonder whether you have room for that.

So many people take a middle path. They speak just enough truth to feel honest, but not enough to disrupt. They hint. They allude. They test the waters with careful language. That isn't dishonesty.

It's survival.

What changes slowly is your understanding of what silence costs in return. Not speaking doesn't protect you the way you hoped. The tension you avoid externally accumulates internally. The words you swallow don't disappear. They show up later as irritability, distance, fatigue that rest doesn't touch.

Silence has been asking something of you too.

Sometimes you take the risk anyway—and the hardest version isn't rejection. It's the moment your words land without response. The room goes quiet. No one follows you. No one pushes back either. The agenda continues, leaving your truth suspended in the air like something misplaced.

It takes courage to speak again after that.

And yet, even when truth doesn't change the outcome, it changes you. You feel less divided. Less like you're managing two versions of yourself: the competent responder and the human being underneath. You don't feel lighter exactly.

You feel more aligned.

Over time you begin to redefine courage. Not as saying everything, everywhere, all at once, but as refusing to participate in your own erasure. As choosing moments where honesty is worth the risk. As learning where your truth can land and be held, and where it will be neutralized. You stop offering your most vulnerable observations to people who treat them as inconveniences. That isn't retreat.

It's stewardship.

You also notice something else: courage is contagious. When one person speaks honestly and survives it, others take note. When truth is named and not punished—even quietly—the risk calculus shifts. The field doesn't transform overnight. It changes at the edges, in tone before policy, in language before structure.

That's how truth starts to travel.

Not as a campaign. Not as a confrontation. As recognition passed hand to hand.

You say something honest in a meeting—small, precise. "That one stayed with me." "I understand the decision, but it cost more than we're naming." Nothing dramatic happens. No argument. No applause. The agenda continues.

Later someone catches you near the door. "Thanks for saying that," they say. "I thought it was just me."

That's how it starts.

Truth travels because it gives people language for what they already know. It doesn't persuade as much as it interrupts isolation. It takes something that felt private and makes it shared. At first the change is subtle. People don't suddenly speak freely everywhere. They don't overshare. They don't stop being careful.

What changes is the tone.

Conversations get less polished and more exact. People stop rushing to reassure and start listening for what's actually being said.

Moral discomfort becomes something that can be named without immediately being managed. The work doesn't get easier.

It gets more honest.

You begin to see that honesty doesn't weaken the field. It strengthens it by removing the pressure to pretend. People stay longer when they don't have to disappear to belong. People leave with less damage when they're allowed to say why. People trust each other more when reality doesn't have to be edited for acceptability.

You notice it in recovery, too. When cost is named, it doesn't linger as bitterness or withdrawal. It doesn't leak out sideways as cynicism. It has somewhere to land. Gratitude changes, too. Thanks feel less hollow when they don't replace what was difficult. Being seen includes being thanked, not erased by it.

Truth doesn't spread evenly. Some rooms stay resistant. Some leaders remain uncomfortable. Some teams continue to run on silence because that's what keeps things moving. Truth doesn't force itself into those spaces.

It waits.

Then it finds a crack: a late-night conversation after a response, a quiet admission from someone who rarely speaks, a leader naming uncertainty instead of covering it with confidence. These moments are small.

They accumulate.

Eventually you hear new sentences in the field—sentences that don't solve anything but make staying possible.

"That makes sense that it stayed with you."
"I don't think that was wrong to feel."
"We can acknowledge the cost even if we can't change the outcome."

The system hasn't been dismantled. The constraints haven't disappeared. The decisions still land imperfectly.

But the fiction begins to loosen: the fiction that the system is cost-free, that strength requires silence, that professionalism means invisibility.

By the end of this chapter, nothing has been resolved, and that is intentional. What has changed is permission: permission to trust your own experience, permission to believe that noticing cost does not make you disloyal or weak, permission to speak honestly even when the answer remains the same.

Silence has already taken enough.

The truth doesn't have to arrive like a rupture. It can arrive the way so much else arrives in this work: quietly, steadily, through recognition—until what was unspeakable becomes simply real, and reality becomes shareable.

That isn't the end of the conversation.

It's the beginning of a different one.

Chapter 14—**Staying, Leaving, and Staying Changed**

The False Choice

For a long time, the story sounds simple.

You either stay or you leave.

You're either committed or you're done.

Strong enough or worn out.

Still called to the work or finally ready to admit it took too much from you.

It's a tidy story.

It's also wrong.

The false choice shows up quietly, usually in moments when you're already tired. Someone asks how long you plan to keep doing this. A colleague mentions stepping back and frames it as "not being able to handle it anymore." A leader praises those who've been around the longest, as if longevity alone were proof of integrity. You absorb the message without realizing it:

Staying means something about who you are.

Leaving means something else.

There isn't much room in between.

At first, the binary helps. It gives you a way to orient yourself. A clear identity. A sense of belonging. You know where you stand because you're still here. You're still responding. You're still willing to say yes.

That clarity matters, especially early on.

Later, it becomes a constraint.

You begin to notice how people talk about leaving. Not openly. Not neutrally. Even when the tone is kind, the implication tends to remain: leaving happens when staying is no longer possible. Rarely is it framed as a choice made with clarity.

And the false choice misses the most obvious thing your experience keeps proving:

You have already changed.

The work has shaped how you see the world. You notice vulnerability faster. You track power differently. You understand how systems fail people in predictable ways. You hear certain phrases and know exactly what they will cost on the ground.

It has shaped you, too. You are more careful with hope. More aware of limits. More attuned to the moral weight of small decisions. None of this is accidental. None of it is neutral.

Staying has never meant standing still. Staying has always meant adapting.

The question you've begun to ask isn't Can I stay?

It's Who am I becoming if I do?

This is where the binary starts to fray, because leaving isn't the only alternative to staying unchanged.

There is another path, less visible and less discussed:

Staying changed.

Staying changed doesn't look dramatic. From the outside, you're still here. You still respond. You still show up to meetings, carry responsibility, make decisions. What's different is internal. You no longer pretend the work is cost-neutral. You no longer measure commitment by how much you can absorb without speaking. You no longer confuse endurance with integrity.

You become more selective. You say no more often. You protect parts of yourself that used to be available by default. You let certain ambitions go. You refuse certain roles, even when you're capable of them.

To some people, this looks like disengagement.

It isn't.

It's discernment.

You also begin to notice that leaving, when it happens, is rarely the opposite of staying. It's often a continuation of the same attention. The same care that once kept you present now tells you that presence requires distance. The same moral clarity that guided your decisions in the field now guides a different decision.

Leaving becomes not an escape, but a boundary.

If you frame leaving as failure, people stay longer than they should, sacrificing parts of themselves they didn't mean to give up. If you frame staying as the only honorable option, you erase the cost paid by those who do it quietly.

Both stories flatten reality.

By the end of this part, the binary no longer holds.

Staying is not automatically noble.

Leaving is not automatically failure.

Both can be acts of integrity.

What matters is not the direction of the choice, but the quality of attention behind it—whether you are moving toward coherence or away from it, whether you are remaining visible to yourself.

Staying Is Not Static

Staying is often described as if it were a single decision.

You stayed.
You didn't quit.
You're still here.

The language makes it sound settled, resolved, complete.

Your experience tells you otherwise.

Staying is not one choice made once. It is a series of adjustments made over time, often without ceremony or clarity. You don't decide to stay forever. You decide to stay this response. This season. This role. And then you decide again.

Sometimes without realizing you've decided at all.

Early on, staying is simple. You show up. You say yes. You trust the structure to tell you where you're needed and what's expected. Training and policy and leadership carry the moral weight of decisions.

This works, for a while.

Then the work gets closer.

As you gain experience, staying requires discernment. You begin to notice which roles leave you steadier and which ones hollow you out. Which environments allow you to remain human and which ones quietly require you to flatten yourself. Which compromises you can live with and which ones linger.

You rarely talk about this directly. It sounds too subjective. Too personal. Too hard to justify in a culture that values availability and adaptability. So you translate your choices into acceptable language.

"I'm better suited here."
"This fits my skill set."
"I can be more effective in this role."

All of that may be true.

It's also cover for a deeper question: Can I stay without losing something I can't get back?

Staying begins to involve subtraction. You stop volunteering for certain assignments. You decline leadership roles that once felt affirming but now feel too exposed. You choose positions with clearer boundaries, even if they carry less prestige.

From the outside, it can look like pulling back.

From the inside, it feels like staying responsibly.

This is where staying gets misunderstood. People assume the ones who stay longest can tolerate the most, have the thickest skin, are least affected. Often, the opposite is true. The people who stay well are usually those who have learned to be affected selectively. They allow themselves to feel, but not everywhere. They engage deeply, but not indiscriminately. They know when to step forward and when to step back.

They are not unchanged.

They are calibrated.

They don't stay by denying reality. They stay by negotiating with it.

Some seasons ask more than others. Some responses hit closer to home. Some decisions cross lines you didn't know you had until they were tested. Staying means revisiting your limits, not setting them once and assuming they'll hold.

Your questions change.

Not "Can I handle this?"
But "What will this require of me?"
And "Am I willing to give that right now?"

These questions don't come with guilt.

They come with responsibility.

There is loss here. Staying changed often means letting go of certain identities. You may no longer be the person who can jump into any role at any time. You may no longer be the one who absorbs the hardest conversations because you're "good at it." You may no longer be endlessly available to mentor without replenishment.

You grieve these shifts quietly.

They mattered to you. They were part of how you understood your value.

What replaces them is less visible. You become someone who knows when enough is enough. Someone who can read the moral temperature of a room and decide whether to engage or conserve. Someone who understands staying requires sustainability, not sacrifice without limit.

This kind of staying doesn't get celebrated much. It doesn't look heroic.

It looks steady.

And it can feel lonely. You don't quite fit the narratives anymore. You're not untouched enough to be idealized, and you're not burned out enough to be warned about. You occupy a middle space that often goes unnamed.

And yet, this is where many people actually live.

They stay, but differently than they did before. They carry the work with more awareness and less illusion. They are still committed, but no longer unquestioning.

By the end of this part, staying no longer looks like a fixed identity.

It looks like a practice—one that requires attention, adjustment, and honesty over time.

Staying, when done well, is not about proving strength.

It is about maintaining coherence.

Leaving Is Not Failure

Most people don't leave in a moment of drama.

They leave quietly.

They finish a response and don't sign up for the next one. They shift into a different role without making an announcement. They say they're "taking a break" and don't specify when it will end.

From the outside, it can look like fading.

From the inside, it often feels like relief mixed with grief.

The dominant story doesn't make much room for this. Leaving is usually framed as what happens when someone can't handle the work anymore—a personal limit reached, burnout that wasn't managed well enough. Even when this framing is gentle, it's still narrow. It reduces a complex decision to a failure of endurance.

You've seen how unfair that is.

When you talk with people who left intentionally, the story sounds different. They don't describe being overwhelmed in the way the narrative expects. They describe noticing a mismatch that wouldn't resolve. They describe staying long enough to understand the cost clearly, and then deciding that continuing would require too much erosion.

They didn't leave because they stopped caring.

They left because they cared and wanted to remain themselves.

Leaving often comes after staying changed has been tried. People adjust roles. Reduce exposure. Set boundaries. Advocate for shifts in culture. They do the honest work of staying thoughtfully.

Sometimes, that's enough.

Sometimes, it isn't.

When leaving comes from this place, it is not reactive.

It is deliberate.

The hardest part of leaving is often not the decision itself.

It's the meaning assigned to it by others.

"They needed better self-care."
"They just couldn't handle it anymore."
"It was too much for them."

These explanations are neat. They protect the system from having to ask harder questions. They relocate the burden back into the individual and let the structure remain unexamined.

Leaving also has its own internal work. Even when the decision feels right, it can feel like betrayal—of colleagues, of people you served, of a version of yourself who believed this work would be lifelong.

You grieve not just the role, but the identity attached to it.

Who are you if you're not this person anymore?

And yet, over time, you begin to see what remains. Skills remain. Values remain. The capacity to witness without turning away remains. Often, those things become easier to access once they aren't being traded daily for compromise.

Leaving doesn't erase what you gave.

It can preserve what you might have lost.

By the end of this part, leaving is no longer a failure state.

It is one possible response to sustained moral demand.

It sits alongside staying changed as another way people try to remain coherent in work that asks a lot of them.

Who You Are Without the Role

For a long time, the role gives you shape. It tells you where to be, what to carry, how to speak. It gives you language for your days and structure for your purpose. When people ask what you do, the answer comes easily, and it means something—to them and to you.

Over time, the role becomes more than a function.

It becomes a way of understanding yourself.

This is why both staying and leaving can feel disorienting. If you stay long enough, the role can begin to crowd out other parts of you. Decisions get filtered through it. Relationships bend around it. Even rest becomes instrumental—something you do so you can return.

If you leave, the absence can feel louder than expected. The calendar opens up. The urgency drops away. The familiar questions stop coming.

Who are you now?

This question isn't a crisis.

It's an invitation.

But it doesn't feel like one at first.

It takes time to relearn yourself outside of urgency. To feel the difference between being needed and being whole. To notice which habits were practical in the field but unnecessary everywhere else. To let your nervous system recalibrate from constant readiness.

Gradually, something else emerges: the realization that the work shaped you, but it doesn't own you. The values that brought you into the work don't disappear when a role shifts. They show up differently—in how you listen, how you notice power, how you respond to suffering without needing to fix it.

The work taught you many things.

It does not get to define all of you.

And you don't have to wait until you leave to reclaim yourself. Those who stay can hold the role more lightly, even while performing it well. They can refuse to let usefulness be the sole measure of worth. They can build lives that do not orbit entirely around response. They can remain visible to themselves.

This is the integration that makes staying or leaving sustainable: not clinging to the role, not rejecting it either—letting it be one chapter in a larger life.

By the end of this chapter, the question has shifted.

It is no longer Should I stay or leave?

It is How do I live with integrity, wherever I am?

That question doesn't demand one answer.

It demands attention.

And attention—unlike endurance—is something you can keep offering without disappearing.

Chapter 15—**What Remains**

After the Work Is Done

When people talk about the end of disaster work, they often imagine an ending that doesn't exist. They picture a final deployment, a clear transition, a moment when the work is finished and its effects can be neatly set down—as if you step out of the field and everything that mattered there stays behind, contained by geography and time. That's not how it happens. What remains is not dramatic. It's quieter than that.

The work does not end when you leave a site. It doesn't end when the response closes or the shelter shuts down or the command structure dissolves. It doesn't end when you turn in a badge or stop answering the phone. It ends in pieces, and some of those pieces never fully leave.

You notice this first in small, almost ordinary ways. A news story catches your attention faster than it used to. A certain kind of weather makes you alert without thinking. You notice evacuation routes in places you've never worked. You track exits automatically. You clock who looks lost in crowded rooms. None of this feels like trauma. It feels like knowledge that has settled into your body.

You also notice what doesn't fade: the faces you can still see, the voices you can still hear, the moments when you stood in front of someone and knew that what you were offering was not enough, but it was what you had. These memories don't ask to be resolved. They ask to be acknowledged.

There is a temptation, especially once the work is no longer active, to ask what it was all for—to measure impact, tally outcomes, decide whether the cost was justified. These questions are understandable, but they are incomplete. The work was not only about what was fixed or restored or improved. It was about how people were treated in moments when they were most exposed, and whether care was present even when solutions were limited. Those moments matter in ways that don't translate cleanly into metrics.

What remains is often relational. You remember how it felt to be trusted by someone you'd just met, how quickly intimacy formed under pressure, how responsibility arrived without invitation and stayed longer than expected. You remember the weight of being believed. That kind of experience changes how you understand human connection, and you don't forget it.

What also remains is moral. You carry a clearer sense of where systems break down. You see how policy decisions land on bodies. You recognize how easily harm can be normalized when it's framed as necessary. This knowledge doesn't make you cynical; it makes you precise. You are less easily reassured by explanations that smooth over impact, and you listen for what's missing as much as for what's said. This is not only a burden. It can also feel like responsibility.

There is grief in what remains—not only for what was lost in disasters, but for the versions of yourself that existed before the work reshaped you. For the innocence that allowed you to believe some things would be simpler than they are, and for the certainty that endurance alone was enough. You don't need to romanticize that loss, and you don't need to minimize it. Grief remains because care was real.

There is also gratitude, but not the shallow kind that skips over cost. It's the deeper kind that holds complexity: gratitude for people who stood beside you, for moments of clarity in the middle of confusion, for times when care landed even imperfectly. This gratitude doesn't erase what was hard. It sits alongside it.

As time passes, you begin to see that what remains is not just memory. It's orientation. The work has tuned your attention, sharpened your ethical instincts, and made certain compromises impossible to ignore and certain values impossible to abandon. You may no longer be responding, but you are still responding to the world differently.

This can feel lonely. People who haven't done this work may not understand why certain things matter to you now, why some conversations feel insufficient, why you resist easy narratives about resilience or recovery. You learn to choose carefully where you tell certain stories. You don't need everyone to understand. You need a few people who recognize what you're talking about without explanation.

What remains also includes responsibility for how the story of the work is told. You know how easily it can be simplified, how quickly responders can be turned into symbols rather than people, how often cost is erased in favor of heroism or efficiency. You feel a quiet obligation to tell the truth more carefully—not to sensationalize, not to accuse, but to refuse distortion.

This chapter isn't here to summarize or conclude. It's here to slow things down and acknowledge that endings in this work are never clean. That's not a failure of closure; it's a reflection of how deeply the work intersects with who you are. What remains is not something you have to justify. You don't owe proof that the work mattered, or an accounting of cost versus benefit, or a narrative that makes everything make sense. You owe yourself honesty.

In the next part, we will turn toward responsibility—not as burden, but as inheritance. For now, it's enough to say this: the work may end, but what it gives you, and what it takes, does not simply disappear. Learning how to live with what remains is its own kind of response.

The Weight You Inherit

Responsibility doesn't end when the work does; it changes shape. While you're actively responding, responsibility is concrete. You know what needs to be done, who needs you, what decisions are yours to make. The urgency organizes your attention. The structure tells you where to stand. Afterward, responsibility becomes quieter and harder to define because it no longer arrives with instructions.

You inherit knowledge—not just technical knowledge, but moral knowledge. You know how quickly people fall through gaps. You know how often systems rely on individuals to absorb consequences that were never meant to be personal. You know how fragile dignity can be when it's mediated by process. This knowledge doesn't announce itself as responsibility; it simply changes how you move through the world. You notice it when someone explains a decision with confidence that feels misplaced, when you hear the missing pieces, when you recognize harm being reframed as inevitability. You don't always speak, but you notice, and noticing carries weight.

There is also the inheritance of voice. You've been in rooms where decisions were made. You've seen how language shapes outcomes, and you understand how certain phrases justify certain actions. You can't unknow that. Sometimes you feel a pull to intervene when you hear similar patterns elsewhere—to ask a question that disrupts the narrative, to remind people consequences don't stay abstract. This isn't activism in the dramatic sense. It's ethical reflex.

The weight of this inheritance is uneven. Some days it feels manageable; other days it surprises you. You catch yourself reacting strongly to things that seem minor to others and wonder if you're overreacting. You're not. You're responding from a deeper field of reference.

There is also responsibility toward memory. You carry stories that do not belong to you alone—stories of people at their most vulnerable, who trusted you with fragments of their lives. You did not promise to remember them, and yet you do. Remembering isn't replaying events; it's refusing to let those experiences be erased or simplified. This kind of memory can feel isolating because you can't share it freely. Some details are not yours to tell. Some moments would be misunderstood outside the context of the work. You learn to carry them with care, and that care is part of the inheritance.

You also inherit responsibility toward yourself, and this may be the hardest part. You know what sustained moral demand does to people. You've seen what happens when cost goes unnamed for too long. You understand how easily commitment turns into erosion. You can't pretend ignorance anymore. You're responsible for how you respond to that knowledge in your own life—not as self-protection at all costs, but as honesty. Recognizing you're approaching limits isn't failure, and your well-being isn't separate from the ethics of the work. How you carry yourself now is part of what remains.

There is a collective dimension too. You are part of a community of people who have seen similar things, even if your experiences didn't overlap directly. You recognize each other through language, through pauses, through what doesn't need to be explained. You may feel responsibility to that community even when you're no longer formally part of it: to speak truthfully when the work is misrepresented, to support those still in it when you can, to resist narratives that erase cost in the name of efficiency or heroism. This responsibility is not a demand; it's an orientation. You can engage it differently at different times. It doesn't expire.

Meaning leaves traces. The inheritance of this work is not a burden you have to carry perfectly. There is no right way to hold it. There is only the ongoing practice of noticing when it is asking something of you, and deciding—consciously—how to respond. In the next part, we will turn toward repair—not as fixing what can't be fixed, but as living in a way that allows what remains to settle without hardening. The goal is not to be free of the work. It's to be in right relationship with what it left behind.

Living With It Without Hardening

There is a moment, often later than you expect, when you realize what remains has begun to settle—not resolve, not disappear, but settle. The edges aren't as sharp. The memories don't intrude as often. You can move through ordinary days without feeling constantly pulled back into response mode. Life widens again, and still something is different.

The risk at this stage is not collapse. It's hardening. You've seen it before: people who stay close to suffering for too long sometimes protect themselves by narrowing. They become efficient, skeptical, less available to complexity. They call it realism. Sometimes it is. Sometimes it's armor that's grown too thick to feel through. You don't want that—not because you want to stay open to everything, but because you know what it costs to close down completely.

Living with what remains requires a different kind of care than surviving the work itself. During response, care is urgent—rest, boundaries, rotation, getting through the day. Afterward, care becomes slower and less directive. There is no checklist, no supervisor reminding you to step back. You have to notice for yourself when something is beginning to stiffen.

You notice it in small ways: when sarcasm becomes easier than curiosity; when impatience shows up where compassion used to live; when you dismiss complexity because you're tired of holding it. These moments don't mean you're failing. They mean something is asking for attention.

Hardening often masquerades as wisdom. You tell yourself you've seen too much to be surprised anymore, that you know how things really work, that optimism is naïve and idealism unrealistic. Some of this is earned. The danger is when it becomes the only story you tell.

You begin to understand that staying soft is not the same as staying exposed. Softness, in this sense, isn't openness to harm. It's permeability: the ability to let experience move through you without getting stuck or turning corrosive. This kind of softness takes practice, and one way you practice is by allowing complexity without rushing to judgment. You stop forcing every experience into a category and let things be mixed: necessary and harmful, meaningful and costly, true and insufficient. This doesn't make decisions easier. It makes them more honest.

You also practice by choosing where to invest your care. You don't owe everyone access to the parts of you shaped by the work. Some people won't understand them. Some will try to simplify them into something easier to hold. You learn to choose audiences carefully—not because you're guarded, but because you're respectful of what the work gave you.

Another way you resist hardening is by staying connected to your body. So much of this work trained you to override bodily signals in the name of urgency. Afterward, your body has to be re-invited. You notice when tension lingers, when sleep doesn't come easily, when breath stays shallow without reason. These aren't problems to fix quickly. They're information.

You also learn you don't have to provide closure for anyone else. People want reassurance that you're okay now, that you've moved on, that the work is behind you. They mean well. You're allowed to be ongoing.

Living with what remains includes allowing joy back in without guilt. You may hesitate to enjoy things fully, as if doing so would betray what you've seen or mean forgetting. It doesn't. Joy doesn't erase moral knowledge. It keeps it from calcifying.

Repair doesn't look like resolution. It looks like balance—dynamic balance that shifts as life shifts. You stop trying to get it right once and for all and instead stay responsive. There is humility in this. You accept you won't carry this perfectly, that some days you'll be more brittle than you want to be, that some moments will catch you off guard. You also accept you have resources now you didn't before: you know how to notice misalignment, how to pause, how to ask what something is costing you. Those are not small skills.

By the end of this part, the work is no longer something you're trying to put behind you. It's something you're learning to live alongside—not as a wound, not as a badge, but as a formative experience that shaped you and now asks for stewardship rather than endurance. In the final part of this chapter, we'll turn toward closing—not with answers, but with orientation: what it means to walk forward carrying this work without being consumed by it, and how to let what remains become a source of clarity rather than weight.

Carrying It Forward

There is no clean ending to this work. That is not a failure of closure; it is a reflection of how deeply the work enters people's lives, values, and bodies. Anything that mattered this much was never going to resolve neatly. So the question is not how to put it behind you. It is how to carry it forward.

Carrying it forward does not mean staying in the field forever. It does not mean remaining available to every request or holding yourself in a constant posture of response. It does not mean continuing to absorb cost in silence out of loyalty or habit. Carrying it forward means allowing what you learned to inform how you live now.

You carry it forward when you resist simplifying stories of harm into narratives that make people comfortable, when you refuse to let efficiency be the only measure of success, when you ask—quietly and persistently—who is bearing the cost of a decision. You don't have to be in charge to do this. You just have to be present.

You carry it forward when you notice people being asked to hold too much and you name it gently; when you recognize moral strain before it hardens into cynicism or collapse; when you create space for someone to say, "That didn't sit right," without rushing to fix or explain it away. These moments are small, and they matter.

You carry it forward in how you speak about the work: not as heroism, not as trauma, not as a test of endurance, but as morally demanding labor done by ordinary people inside constrained systems. You tell the truth without sensationalizing. You honor care without romanticizing cost. This kind of storytelling protects the next generation more than any training manual.

You also carry it forward in how you live outside the work. You notice when urgency creeps into places it doesn't belong. You allow yourself to rest without justification. You protect attention, not just time. You refuse to let usefulness be the sole measure of worth. These choices are not selfish. They are corrective.

Carrying it forward includes letting go: letting go of the need for everything to make sense; letting go of the idea you could have done more if you'd just tried harder; letting go of identities that required you to disappear to be effective. What you did mattered, and it does not need to define you completely.

There will be moments when the work resurfaces unexpectedly—a story, a smell, a decision that echoes something familiar. You don't have to push these moments away. You can let them pass through with acknowledgment rather than resistance. They are reminders of what you know, not demands to return.

If there is a legacy to this work, it is not resilience. It is discernment: the ability to see clearly, to choose intentionally, and to remain human in systems that often reward the opposite; the ability to hold care and constraint at the same time without collapsing into denial or despair. That is not something you lose when the work ends. It is something you carry.

You may never feel finished with this work. That doesn't mean you are unfinished. It means you were changed by something that mattered, and being changed does not require repayment. This book does not ask you to stay or to leave. It does not ask you to forgive the work or to condemn it. It asks you to be honest about what it asked of you, and to live in a way that honors that honesty.

When the work is over, what remains is not a debt. It is knowledge, care that has learned its limits, attention shaped by experience. And if you carry it forward with intention rather than obligation, it becomes not a weight, but a guide—walking with you quietly, reminding you of what matters, and when to pause, and when to speak, and when to rest. That is not a conclusion. It is orientation. And it is yours.

A Few Questions to Ponder

These questions are not prompts for action plans or self-assessment.

They are invitations to notice.

You don't need to answer them all. You don't need to answer them quickly. Some may not make sense yet. Others may stay with you longer than you expect.

Let them do what they need to do.

When did you first notice that the work was affecting you in ways you couldn't easily explain?

Not the exhaustion. Not the stress. The subtler shift. The moment you realized something had changed.

What parts of the work have stayed with you the longest, and where do you carry them now?

Which moments return uninvited? Which ones feel unfinished? What do they ask of you, if anything?

Where have you learned to stay silent in order to keep the work moving?

What truths have you learned to edit? What has that silence protected—and what has it cost?

How do you recognize moral strain in your own body or behavior?

Before you name it intellectually, how does it show up physically or relationally?

What have you learned to call "just part of the job" that may deserve a more careful name?

What has been normalized that still doesn't sit right?

In what ways have you adapted in order to stay—and what have those adaptations required you to give up?

Which changes feel like growth? Which ones feel like erosion?

If you've considered leaving, what were you actually responding to?

Was it exhaustion, misalignment, grief, clarity—or something harder to name?

Who are you when the role loosens its grip?

What remains of your identity beyond usefulness, availability, or response?

Where do you find spaces where the truth about the cost can be spoken without being managed?

Who listens without rushing to fix? Where does honesty feel safe enough to land?

What would it mean to live in right relationship with what the work has given you and taken from you?

Not to resolve it. Not to justify it. Just to acknowledge it honestly.

These questions are not meant to push you toward a conclusion.

They are meant to create room.

Room for recognition.
Room for compassion.
Room for a different way of carrying what remains.

You are allowed to take your time with them.

Acknowledgements

This book exists because of people who rarely ask to be named.

It belongs first to the responders who showed up again and again, often without certainty that their presence would be enough, and stayed anyway. Those who listened when there were no answers. Who absorbed anger, grief, and confusion without being allowed to set it down. Who carried decisions they did not make and costs that were never formally acknowledged. You recognized yourselves in these pages long before they were written.

To the disaster survivors who trusted responders with moments of their lives they never planned to share: your dignity shaped this work more than any framework or language ever could. The way you endured, questioned, accepted, resisted, and kept going revealed what care actually means under constraint. I hold those encounters with deep respect.

I am grateful to the colleagues who stayed in conversation when it would have been easier to move on. The ones who said, quietly, "That didn't sit right," or "You're not the only one who feels this." Those moments of recognition mattered more than you know. They are threaded throughout this book.

To leaders who allowed complexity instead of demanding certainty, who made room for truth even when it slowed things down, and who understood that morale is not maintained by silence alone: your courage changed more than policies. It changed people.

This work was shaped by years of serving alongside disaster response partners across faith-based organizations, nongovernmental organizations, and emergency management systems. Each collaboration revealed both the possibility and the cost of care at scale. I am especially grateful to those who trusted me with responsibility, mentorship, and honest disagreement.

I want to acknowledge the communities of practice that quietly sustain responders long after deployments end. The hallway conversations, late-night calls, shared meals, and unstructured check-ins where the real work of meaning-making happens. Much of what is written here was learned in those spaces.

To those who have stepped away from disaster response, whether temporarily or permanently: your leaving mattered. Your clarity mattered. This book resists the idea that endurance is the only measure of integrity because of you.

To those still in the work: may you find language where there was silence, companionship where there was isolation, and permission to name what the work asks of you without having to justify your humanity.

Finally, to the people who made room for this book to be written by not asking me to simplify it, harden it, or turn it into something easier than it is: thank you for trusting the truth to stand on its own.

This book is not a conclusion.

It is an offering.

And it belongs to everyone who has carried the moral weight of this work, whether or not anyone ever named it.

About the Author

Rev. Gregory C. Smith, PhD has spent more than fifteen years responding to disasters, often in places where the damage was visible and the moral weight less so.

He serves on the National Response Team of Presbyterian Disaster Assistance, where he has worked alongside communities and partners in the long arc of recovery following both natural and human-caused disasters. He also provides disaster spiritual care for the American Red Cross, supporting survivors and responders in moments when answers are scarce and presence matters most.

Over the course of more than 100 disaster responses, he has worked in shelters, temporary assistance centers, long-term recovery efforts, and command environments where decisions are made quickly and lived with slowly. His work has placed him at the intersection of care, constraint, and consequence—often as the person asked to translate systems into something human, and to absorb the impact when those systems fall short.

He also serves on the Board of the Iowa VOAD (Voluntary Organizations Active in Disaster), collaborating closely with faith-based organizations, nongovernmental organizations, and state and county emergency managers. Through this work, he has seen both the extraordinary good that coordinated response can achieve and the quiet cost carried by those who sustain it.

This book grew out of lived experience rather than theory. It was written for responders who know the work from the inside, who recognize the moments that don't fit easily into training or debriefs, and who have carried questions that rarely find a place to land.

Rev. Smith believes deeply in disaster response as an expression of care and solidarity. He also believes that caring work done inside constrained systems leaves marks that deserve to be named, not managed away.

He lives with a lasting respect for those who continue to show up, those who have stepped back, and those who are still figuring out what the work has asked of them—and what it has given in return.

www.ingramcontent.com/pod-product-compliance
Lightning Source LLC
LaVergne TN
LVHW052325200926
848481LV00002B/673
* 9 7 9 8 3 8 5 2 8 0 6 2 9 *